Praise for *A Fortunate ...*

Grady Birdsong's family history is Americana at its best— the stories of two families, each unique in its own evolution, and yet both are typical and characteristic of those hardworking people who made America great.

A Fortunate Passage: Two Families' Journey into the Heartland is one of the best family narratives I have read—a story that will command the attention of both amateur historians and those interested in genealogical research.

The author has done a superb job tracing the roots on one side of his family from before the American Revolution and through the Civil War to the present day. His research on the other side took him back to the Volga Delta to rediscover links to a Russian-German heritage, ancestors whose journey to the Great Heartland is a tale that will inspire a wide audience.

—**Dan Guenther,** genealogical researcher and author of *Glossy Black Cockatoos*, the 2010 Colorado Authors' League Award selection for Genre Fiction

A Fortunate Passage is a loving tribute to the grandparents who inspired a young Grady with their values, struggles, and lessons of life that most of us rarely discover. The faded family photos of that early couple; a deserted, weather-worn farmhouse and barn; and an ancient car or train come back to life in his exceptional testimonial to his own greatest generation of Americans.

—**Robert L. Fischer, Colonel, USMC (Ret.),** author, U.S. Naval Academy graduate, former adviser to the Vietnamese Marine Corps, and lecturer on Strategy and Tactics of the Insurgent, Naval War College

Praise for *A Fortunate Passage* continued

A Fortunate Passage captures the true American pioneering spirit. Grady T. Birdsong tenderly weaves detailed imageries of life for his ancestors while tracing his family lineage in this obvious labor of love. The reader is delicately enlightened to the significant role farmlands, the harvesting of wheat and the growth of the American railroads held in forming the heartland of this nation. Alongside the Birdsong family, all Americans should be proud. May future generations be ingenious enough to appreciate and inherit the characteristics of their family heritage, thanks to the efforts of Grady T. Birdsong! *A Fortunate Passage* is truly an invaluable family gift, surely to be cherished for generations to come.

—**Carron Barrella,** author of *More Than 36 Days: Four Ordinary Men Face Extraordinary Circumstances*

"The author's research on his grandfather's railroad career is both well-researched and very readable. His description of his grandfather working around the railroad and riding in the cab of a steam locomotive is detailed down to a photograph of one of the engines he ran."

—**Charlie Duckworth,** Senior Director, eCommerce (retired), Union Pacific Railroad

A FORTUNATE PASSAGE

Two Families' Journey Into the Heartland

GRADY T. BIRDSONG

GTB 2010

A Fortunate Passage
Two Families' Journey Into the Heartland

Library of Congress Number: 2012912680

Printed in the United States of America
ISBN 978-1-62137-065-9 (softcover);
     978-1-62137-070-3 (electronic copy).

Statue of Volga-German families is an oil-photo (digital). The statue was carved by a local area artist, Pete Felten Jr., and is dedicated to the original hardworking settlers of Herzog, Kansas (later renamed Victoria). This statue can be viewed at the St. Fidelis Catholic Church, "Cathedral of the Plains," 900 Cathedral, Victoria, Kansas 67671. Permission was obtained to use this statue photo, courtesy of St. Fidelis Catholic Church.

www.GradyTBirdsong.com

Table of Contents

Acknowledgments

I wrote this book to honor my grandparents and document my good memories of them. I feel a debt of gratitude for their unselfish handing down of the traditional foundations and examples for my family in the areas of character, sincerity, aspiration, faith, honesty, and duty. This history cannot tell their complete story, but is intended to give future generations a glimpse of what they encountered, how they were raised, how they lived, what their challenges were, and what they were like as a father, mother, grandfather, and grandmother during their *fortunate passage.* Woven throughout this narrative are sections of history and some analysis of the times I was able to research and mesh with the applicable subject matter. I felt this would give the family reader and the casual reader insights into my grandparents' lives and the lives of other people during this generation.

This book is a good-faith effort to reconstruct the story of my grandparents with information from remaining family members who chose to help. I sought out and culled the stories about Grandma and Grandpa from those who would share. All views expressed in this book are solely those of the author. This presentation is as correct and honest as I understand and know it.

I want to thank the following people and institutions for assisting me with this project:

Pamela K. Birdsong (my wife and content editor)

Hiram M. Birdsong (my father)

W. Jean Birdsong (my mother)

Rhea L. Birdsong-Heskett (my sister)

Barbara J. Birdsong-Hutcheson (my sister)

Karen Birdsong-Madorin (my cousin and principal editor)

Dean J. Birdsong (my father's cousin and family researcher)

Donald and Marilyn Hergert (my father's cousins and family researchers)

Lou Ann Giesick-Crossland-Deitz (daughter of my great-uncle and great-aunt)

Craig and Linda Crossland (grandchildren of my great-uncle and great-aunt)

Greg Murphy (friend, business associate, writer, and editor)

Dan Guenther (close friend, USMC Vietnam veteran, author, and editor)

Robert L. Fischer, Colonel, USMC (Ret.), (close friend, author, and U.S. Naval Academy graduate)

Carron Barrella (friend, author, and U.S. Marine)

Bob Glynn (family friend in Hoisington, Kansas)

Joe Johnson (past town resident of Hoisington, Kansas)

Mike Madden (my boyhood friend in Hoisington, Kansas)

Patty Nicholas (Fort Hays State University archivist, Hays, Kansas)

Charlie Duckworth (senior director, Union Pacific Railroad, and author)

Steven W. Engerrand (assistant director, Georgia Archives)

Sherri Stahl (American Historical Society of Germans from Russia Village Coordinator, Portland, Oregon)

Nick Zelinger (NZ Graphics, cover artwork and design)

Joyce Miller (copyright-permission editor)

Alexi Paulina (final editor)

Clark Johnson (county historian, Troup County, Georgia)

MoPac Historical Society (Missouri Pacific Railroad)

United States Railroad Retirement Board, Chicago, Illinois

U.S. Army Heritage and Education Center, Carlisle, Pennsylvania

New York Public Library, New York, New York

National Archives and Records Administration, Atlanta, Georgia

Kansas Trails Website, Peggy Thompson (Webmaster)

Oklahoma Ag in the Classroom (www.agclassroom.org/ok)

Kansas State historical Society, Topeka, Kansas (State Archives)

Rush County Historic Society, Judith Reynolds (VP – Curator), La Crosse, Kansas

Saint Fidelis Catholic Church, Victoria, Kansas

I have to point out that I very much appreciate the many hours of endeavor that my dear cousin Karen Birdsong-Madorin, a retired English teacher in central Kansas, put into this book. Even though she has declined all praise, I truly feel she owns a part of creating this book.

Prologue

Traveling through the wheat fields of central and western Kansas, one cannot help but notice the pillars of stone fence posts rimming the section lines of endless, open farm ground. These *monuments of the past* are slowly disappearing with time, but they were once a proud symbol of determined but plain beginnings. These mute landmarks are reminders of an inheritance that is beyond value and purchase. This inheritance, passing silently from one generation to the next, remains intact within the family. It is a Spartan self-reliance and a trust in God of which I speak. It is the story of my family coming to a new land—a story that began in the nineteenth century.

After I read the excellent family genealogy researched and written by my father's cousin, Commander Dean John Birdsong, USN (Ret.), he urged me to research and compose a compilation of facts, history, and family stories. In addition, I am presenting documents regarding Grandfather and Grandmother Birdsong's families. I decided to share what I have discovered through interviews, various family documents, heirlooms, and historical research, and to publish them for the benefit of family members and others.

Why document the family history? My grandmother told me many stories when I was a young boy, and I was awestruck by her lessons about the past. She particularly held my attention when sharing her vivid memories of growing up on a wheat farm and the very hard times she endured. She told me stories of her struggle to raise her family and deal with my grandfather's dying a tragic death from a ruptured appendix at such a young age. Her story was, of course, a selective view, considering the austerity in which her family existed. Nevertheless, I was eager to hear those memories and accounts of sacrifice.

I marveled at her (our) family's determination to endure and succeed despite many challenges. I admired her humble attitude of faith, determination, and work ethic. It set the stage for me to accept the hard work and intense times I would face.

Each written narrative, verbal story, photo, artifact, document, will, deed, etc., left behind is a part of the overall history of not only our family, but also the immediate society of that time. These reflect on the genuine nature and values of the family members and their society. This compilation of family information bequeaths the legacy handed down from this generation. Each story documents the blending of the Birdsong and Giesick families.

I observed and received from my parents and grandparents a love for and allegiance to God, family, and country. Americans are blessed with the good fortune of living in the greatest experiment of government and nation since the beginning of time—One Nation Under God. Some might challenge me, but I will never change my mind on this undeniable accounting of the United States as I learned about it and continue to discover its rich history. I choose to rise above social fear and politics. It was my parents, grandparents, and their parents that helped build this great nation with their sweat, toil, and efforts, however large or small that may seem to the reader. This history weaves a chronicle of these American values. Each small story intertwined with others completes the larger story and melds this narrative into the rich history of this nation. This story tells of the glue that bonds together a robust, good family that struggled to succeed in both good and bad times and records their *passage.*

In reading Dean Birdsong's work, *The Sixth Generation of Birdsong Families in America*, I came across a technique used in a sworn State of Alabama affidavit by a past direct-line relative to convey family information in a factual and historical fashion to preserve it for future family and thus make it as authoritative as is possible. This was a sworn statement before an official of the court. It reads as follows, and I will use this formality of technique to begin this writing:

"Before me, the undersigned authority, personally appeared Herbert Troy Birdsong, who, after being duly sworn, deposes and says as follows..." Herbert Troy was a resident of Boaz, Alabama (near Huntsville), and is buried at the Beulah Baptist Cemetery in Marshall County, Alabama.

Thus...I am Grady T. Birdsong and a resident of Broomfield, Jefferson County, Colorado. I am over the age of 19 years, of sound mind, and have full, complete, and personal knowledge of all those matters set forth herein. I am of the advanced age of 66 years, sound mind and recall, and I feel it important to document for the record the following writings of this Birdsong family genealogy. The following information about my grandparents and their children is an accumulation of interviews, verbal stories, pictures, artifacts, documents, historical readings, and general information I have quilted together to tell their story from a grandson's perspective.

This family history begins in two very distinct and faraway places on this globe and eventually brings together a man and woman from diverse backgrounds and cultures. On one side, the ethnic German family emigrates from the Volga River colonies of Russia through an East Coast portal and settles in remote, hostile, arid grasslands on the high plateaus of the central United States. This was at a time when the land was just becoming habitable— a time of new settlement.

On the other side, a young, orphaned son of a country doctor travels from the southern mountains of Georgia in search of a new life as he follows his older brother to the high plains that the Native Americans, the *Kansa,* called home. This family history takes place during the concomitant end of the industrial revolution and culminates with a new generation of family at the beginning of the information revolution.

Hard work, *bartering*, and *the Depression* were the watchwords I became familiar with as I matured. These words were the essence of my grandfather's and grandmother's psyches. Everything possible was saved; everything that could be was reused or rebuilt, and Grandmother could make leftover meals taste like a five-star gourmet meal. Nothing was wasted. My Uncle Dwight, her youngest son, at one time accused my Grandmother Martha of being so frugal that she was hoarding and saving ice cubes!

Grandfather Hiram (his nickname, explained later) was for most of his life a railroad man. First he was a fireman, and then he was an engineer on the steam locomotives of the Missouri Pacific that traversed the rail system of western Kansas from Hoisington to Horace and back in the early 1900s. He was also a devout practitioner in the Masonic Lodge and attained the 32° (a Master of the Royal Secret of the 32 Degree of the Ancient and Accepted Scottish Rite).

He was a man greatly admired. In addition, he was a consummate fisherman of catfish, living for the opportunity to go fishing anytime he could steal away to the Smoky Hill and Saline Rivers of central Kansas. He also was a hunter of small game, a pleasure that was passed on to my father and now to my generation.

His father, Dr. James Christian Birdsong, labored as a country doctor who faithfully served the people of his community in the remote regions of western Georgia in the late 1800s. I am sorry my grandfather did not live long enough for me to get to know him and his life story better, although I heard it many times from my grandmother and other family members. This is my continued story of the long lineage of Birdsongs, traced and researched by Dean John Birdsong back to colonial Virginia, circa late 1600 into the 1700s to the Charles Parish of colonial Virginia (one of the first settlements in America). That parish was located in York County, Virginia, which is near the first settlement of Jamestown and specifically named Poquoson, Virginia. York County was originally named Charles River County for King Charles I of England. It was one of the eight "shires" (Great Britain's administrative districts) formed in

1634. The current naming was finalized in 1643, probably to honor the second son of Charles I.

The research currently being done by Dean on origin of the name *Birdsong* indicates the name is of English origin (perhaps originating in Germany and surfacing in England), even though other nationalities blended into the family along the way. That is where the past family research ends, with no one in the family to date having gone to Europe to find the roots of the European Birdsong name and family. It is known from the history of this first colonial settlement area that a substantial number of the immigrants in Virginia prior to 1640 were from the southern and eastern part of England. When these immigrants arrived, the local inhabitants, governed by a chief named Powhatan, greeted them. This Chesapeake Bay topography held approximately 15,000 Native Americans when the first settlers arrived in 1607.

Some history is known about my grandmother's Giesick lineage and their origins in Germany. (It is documented that they were German colonists living in Russia in the Volga River Valley area and were grain farmers.) Her father was Adam Giesick, who was born on November 12, 1865, in the Brunnental area of Russia close to the Volga River.

In 1870, the Czar of Russia decreed that special privileges granted to the German colonist farmers by Catherine II in 1762 were no longer valid. Alarmed, many of the colonists decided to leave the country to look for new homes where they could be free and independent. This was their original intent when they settled in the colonies at the behest of Catherine's grants in the late 1700s. At that time, delegates were sent to South America and North America to investigate the possibilities of colonization. As a result, many went both to Argentina and to western Kansas in the central United States. My great-grandfather, Adam Giesick, came to Kansas through the port of New York* on December 25, 1886, on board the SS Aller, which departed from Bremen, Germany, earlier that December. He had to leave Russian soil before his twenty-first birthday or he would have been conscripted into military service in Russia (as described in a handwritten, photocopied letter passed on to me by my mother and notated, *The Story of the Giesick Family,* by Samuel Giesick, dated April 29, 1974. (Giesick, 1974)

There are many stories of our family that will be explored in this family history. It is my pledge to be as factual as possible, presenting supportive documentation to reinforce the telling of my family's ancestry, journeys, and footprint in a new land.

*Footnote: Ellis Island officially opened on January 1, 1892.

PART I: THE BIRDSONG FAMILY

Chapter 1 ~ Family Origins

To certify this story of my grandparents, Herbert Monroe Birdsong (nicknamed *Hiram*) and Martha (Giesick) Birdsong, I felt it important to give background on local histories along the way, document the family members of both sides in family group charts, and provide supporting documents. This gives the reader a perspective of the origin, character, and depth of this family. I have researched beyond my grandparents' generation looking for pertinent information which would tell our family's story.

Families were quite large in the late 1800s. There were many reasons for extensive families throughout history, but probably the most prominent was that the family was the economic unit of a primarily agricultural nation in the nineteenth and twentieth centuries. This role has diminished in today's society for a variety of reasons, including many technological developments. Thus, it is important to lay down some historical background and geographical information as to origin of family in order to merge, mix, and blend this *fortunate passage* into a clear family history.

Our cousin Dean John Birdsong has diligently and skillfully traced not only the direct line of family back to the Jamestown area of Virginia, but also has compiled an amalgamation of the majority of recorded Birdsongs throughout the beginnings of the United States. He has completed his research through venues of scattered documents such as census records, wills, deeds, local histories, and other writings. He found most of the Birdsongs in the southeastern and southern regions of the United States. In addition to documenting our family's direct line, he provided pedigree charts of the other family lines that will provide (as he states in his two books) a "place to start" for the genealogical researcher for all Birdsongs. I believe he has amassed the most comprehensive genealogical database on the Birdsong name of anyone in the United States.

His latest genealogy of the direct line of our Birdsongs shows a family migration to Georgia (originating from the York County, Virginia, area) and next moving to Brunswick County, Virginia, and then to Oglethorpe County, Georgia. Once in Georgia, our Birdsongs eventually migrated to Upson County, Georgia, and then into Roanoke County, Alabama, and back to Georgia's Troup and Carroll counties and finally Talbot County. (Birdsong D. J., Ancestry & Descendants of My Grandparents Dr. James C. Birdsong MD & Mary L. Weaver, 2010)

Early Western Georgia

During my research, I came across writing from the Georgia area that provides a flavor of the early beginnings and history of the area where our direct family line lived and worked. Written almost a hundred years ago, it lightly touches the surface of that early colonial period. The following excerpts give a rudimentary idea of how the region was settled, setting the stage for our roots in Georgia. It also paints a picture of the steady westerly movement of people that settled the many frontiers of the continental United States.

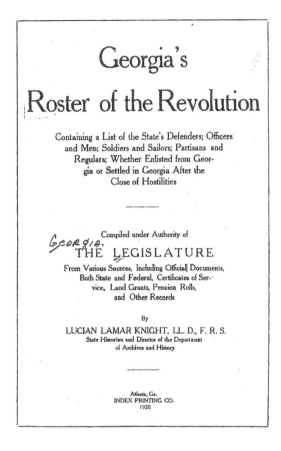

Georgia's
Roster of the Revolution

Containing a List of the State's Defenders; Officers
and Men; Soldiers and Sailors; Partisans and
Regulars; Whether Enlisted from Georgia or Settled in Georgia After the
Close of Hostilities

Compiled under Authority of
Georgia.
THE LEGISLATURE
From Various Sources, Including Official Documents,
Both State and Federal, Certificates of Ser-
vice, Land Grants, Pension Rolls,
and Other Records

By
LUCIAN LAMAR KNIGHT, LL. D., F. R. S.
State Historian and Director of the Department
of Archives and History

Atlanta, Ga.
INDEX PRINTING CO.
1920

Lucian Lamar Knight, LL. D., F.R.S – State Historian
(Lucian Lamar Knight, 1920)

Compiler's Preface – After the lapse of more than a century, the difficulty of compiling a Roster of Georgia troops in the Revolution can be readily imagined. Much of the information which an earlier period might have furnished is now unhappily beyond our reach. Many important records have been lost. To compile an exhaustive roster, therefore, is humanly impossible...

Georgia did not furnish a large body of troops to the Revolutionary struggle. She was the youngest of the English colonies, and, with only a scant population, was situated on the remote southern frontier. Nevertheless, the Georgia contingent gave a good account of itself, whether in the Continental Army or the Home Guard...or in expelling British Regulars.

At the close of hostilities with England, she rewarded her brave defenders with substantial grants of land. To encourage the rapid settlement of her territory, by the best class of immigrants, she offered handsome inducements to the veterans... which led to Georgia... The grants made to these soldiers were called bounties. Thus it came to pass that, while the contributions of Georgia to the army of independence were numerically small, she acquired a vast body of veterans who here found permanent homes; and today there is hardly a State in the Union whose soil is richer in Revolutionary dust.

The earlier land grants were in the nature of Head-Rights. These in time were superseded by grants made under the old Lottery System. Elsewhere, in an article written by the late Secretary of State, Hon. Phillip Cook, the differences between the two methods of distributing land, are fully explained. Records still exist in the Capitol, showing in many instances at least, to whom these lands were deeded. Certificates from superior officers attesting the fidelity of men under them are still preserved; and from sources of information like these, the roster has been obtained. Other helpful sources have been the Pension Rolls of the United States Government, the records of the Federal

War Department, and the reports of the Smithsonian Institution. It is the aim of this roster to include within its survey not only all Georgians who enlisted in the struggle for independence, during the seven years of its continuance, but also all soldiers from other States who settled in Georgia subsequent thereto... (Lucian Lamar Knight, 1920)

This document affirms the aspirations and foundations of the people who settled this area and gives a glimpse of their character. The *bounties* granted to veterans started in earnest the settlement of this wilderness. A people who would venture outside the bounds of firm governance and establish a new life reveal a spirit of individualism with independent and adventurous thinking. In my estimation, only free thinking, courageous, determined, and/or displaced people settle in frontier areas. We know from family history that the earlier direct Birdsong line started in Virginia and found its way to western Georgia. One may speculate that the family could have been influenced in some ways by this migration to the Lottery/Settlement agenda of this new frontier in Georgia. Or could it have been the spirit of carving out a new life in a new and almost unregulated frontier that appealed to them? I believe it was this self-reliant spirit inherent in my grandfather and his older brother, James that explains why they chose to journey into Kansas in the early 1900s. In Lucian Knight's book, no Birdsongs surface on this incomplete, partial roster. One can only guess whether they knew about the land grants, if they qualified, or why they came to Georgia. There are no personal family recollections or records. It is in this spectrum that I develop the known background and present the story of my grandparents, who came together by good fortune into the culture of the times.

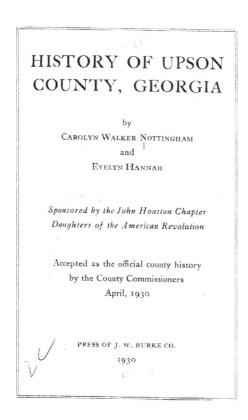

History of Upson County, Georgia (Hannah, 1930)

This unique county historical document chronicles the county close to the homestead of Hiram's grandfather, Edmund Lowe Birdsong, established by census records during the early 1800s. Upson County surrounds the village of Thomaston (now a regional center), and the nearby Flint River serves as the boundary between the two counties. This provides a view of the times, the area, its environs, and some history of settlement.

Court house records must be antedated, and the true beginnings of Upson County must be sought in the primeval solitudes of a prehistoric Georgia. The earliest known inhabitants of this region were Creek Indians, though still further back, in the unrecorded aeons, Upson may have been the home of a still more ancient race known as the Mound Builders. But the matter is purely speculative; the oldest land-marks shed no light upon these lost tribes of the forest...No clue can be found to a race beyond the Creeks. They have bequeathed to us the musical names which still cling to many localities of which, mingling with the roar of waterfalls and with the (not readable) of running waters, recall the Arcadian days of the Red Man... It will be noticed that advancement was ever westward, each new county being just beyond the latest one organized.

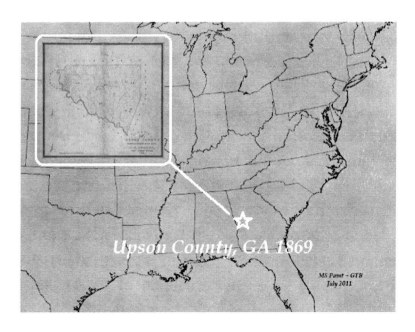

Upson County Map source: http://cdm.sos.state.ga.us
(Georgia, Upson County Map 1869, 1869)

15

During the early years it was determined that a state militia, the forerunner of the National Guard, would be established. There would be one hundred men subject to military duty in each district or county, and muster days would be held in each county where these individuals would drill and hold contests that the whole community would observe in a festival-like atmosphere. The state was a military Division of men, and several districts made up a Brigade. These units were broken down into the county or district population areas, with one-hundred-man rosters. In 1852, Upson County was considered part of the eighth division and second brigade of state militia. Major General James W. Armstrong, of Macon, Georgia, commanded the division, and Brigadier General Davenport Evans of Thomaston, commanded the second brigade.

This Upson County history also includes George L. F. Birdsong, Joseph Birdsong, Edward Birdsong, and James Birdsong—all descendants of earlier Birdsongs from the Virginia area. Their traced family roots start with James and Frances Merritt Birdsong (1726). George L. F. Birdsong is mentioned most frequently in this history. He served as foreman of the Grand Jury in 1859, justice of the Inferior Court from 1849 to 1850, deputy sheriff from 1860 to 1864, and sheriff from 1864 to 1866. (Hannah, 1930)

George Lawrence Forsyth Birdsong, a second cousin to Edmund Lowe Birdsong (Hiram's grandfather), was also known to have served as a captain of the Upson County Guards when the Confederate states called for volunteers in 1863. He returned to his duties as sheriff of the county in 1864. (Birdsong D. J., Ancestry & Descendants of My

Grandparents Dr. James C. Birdsong MD & Mary L. Weaver, 2010)

The Early Settlements

The lure of a new frontier was never far from the thoughts of Americans, no matter what their background. As populations grew along the coast, land increased in value. The pursuit of a better life and new beginnings to the southeast would become very attractive for many after the American Revolution. I found the settling of western Georgia to be quite interesting. The establishment of the few towns and villages in western Georgia was not an easy transformation into the early nineteenth century. In reading the few historical accounts that are available, we find vital cultivations of this beginning society in the writings of Clifford L. Smith:

> *Toward the western border line,*
> *Near Chattahoochee's silver stream,*
> *Where groves of maple, oak and pine*
> *Drive off the sun's too garish beam,*
> *A village sits, amid classic shades.*
>
> —E. Y. Hill from his poem *Georgia*

Many dramatic incidents are to be found in the interesting story of the settlements and organizations of the cities and villages of western Georgia. At times the action of this story is swift and breath-taking, epic in form, depicting the hardships and fierce struggles, also the high courage and valor of the early settlers. With the passage of the years the movement of the story changes to a slower tempo, characteristic of a pastoral life.

As a result of the Indian Springs treaty of 1825 with the Creek Indian Nation, a large area of land between the Flint and Chattahoochee rivers was opened for new settlement. Troup County was one of five areas that allowed settlers into the region around 1827. The area was fertile, forested with plenty of wild game, and the Native Americans were, for the most part, peaceful. Some of the new settlers came into possession of their land by lottery grant and some by purchase. The first early pioneers fashioned log houses from plentiful trees in the countryside. Many of the people who began new lives in this frontier were from Virginia and the Carolinas and were veterans of the American Revolution.

They bartered with the Native Americans who lived in what is now eastern Alabama who wanted corn, chickens, and eggs from the settlers. These Indians would ask for these food items, offering in return handicrafts, moccasins, and other items. The presence of new inhabitants put pressure on the Creek Indians, and the times began to change. Under the treaty there was provision to arrange for the Indians to be moved beyond the Mississippi river. However, some of the more brave and rebellious ones resisted leaving and existed by pillaging from the new settlers. (Smith, 1933)

Clark Johnson, Troup County historian, in an interview provided further insight to the Indians of this area and the times: *The Creeks were not the "native" Indians of this area; their own history tells how they moved in here (around 1500 to1600) and completely massacred the Indian group living here ahead of them. The Treaty of 1825, though challenged and rewritten within the next year or so, gave the Creeks an equivalent amount of land west of the Mississippi which their leaders selected, and in 1826 the State of Georgia (to whom the U.S. gave this land; remember the U.S. government made the Treaty of 1825, because states do not have the authority to make treaties with foreign powers) sent in surveying teams as the Creeks moved over the line into that part of East Alabama still in possession of other Creeks, prior to their moving west. The land was distributed by the State of Georgia beginning in 1827 in a lottery... There was no period of co-habitation here between settlers and Indians. The trade Clifford Smith mentions took place with the Indians in Alabama. Keep in mind, the Alabama Creeks were the Red Sticks (those who opposed the U.S. and white settlement), and the Georgia Creeks were the White Sticks. The White Sticks had sold their lands (some 49 of their chiefs, which was all but one or two of them, signed the sale) and moved into Alabama, preparatory to moving west. When they moved on, the Red Stick Alabama Creeks still lived over the line, and it was those Indians (not the ones who had sold and moved from Georgia) who resented the settlements over in Georgia and are the ones who then launched the Creek Indian War of 1836, which led to their removal from Alabama...which had nothing to do with the voluntary sale and removal from Georgia 10 years previously.* (Johnson C. , 2012)

Cotton eventually became quite important to the South, as was tobacco in the early colonial days. Cotton, like tobacco, debased the soil; therefore the quest for more virgin land to cultivate stimulated the push toward more new land. The new movement into Georgia was encouraged by the practices of what had already been established in the existing states (colonies). Georgia encouraged new settlers with free offerings of the lands it acquired from the Cherokee and Creek Indians. Veterans were given first priority.

This created the beginning of what was termed a "cotton rush." Most of these new frontiersmen came from the mid-Atlantic states, especially Virginia, Maryland, and North Carolina, moving south and then west. Cotton would be a major factor in the way people of the Old South would fashion their lives. With the invention of the cotton gin by Eli Whitney, this new technology would revolutionize the whole agriculture infrastructure of the southern states. It required the labor of many, thus slavery began to expand in the South. They needed many pairs of hands to harvest a crop of cotton, and the southern states focused on cotton because of the newly open lands and the cotton gin.

Cotton was a volatile commodity and the market prices were quite cyclic, rising and falling exponentially throughout the cotton plantation era. Its fluctuating value became the near death of that industry in the Old South in the nineteenth century, as had occurred with tobacco in the eighteenth century. Cotton exhausted the land and played a major role in pushing settlers even further west. The Civil War brought about the end of this way of life.

This gives an adequate but brief glimpse of the travails that faced newcomers to western Georgia and, of course, our

Birdsongs. The written work by Smith explains some of the daily experiences encountered and overcome, with new methods or sometimes just brute force. That brute force was good, old-fashioned hard work.

You hear of white settlers uprooting the Indian tribes throughout America as this nation expanded, but this does not convey the mental picture of the numbers—that is, the raw population numbers. Based on my readings, the number of settlers overwhelmed the number of Native Americans during these times. Free-spirited people exiting from previously established colonies and the eastern seaboard moved *en masse* to this new area, quickly outnumbering the various tribes that dotted the landscape and pushing them westward. The ratio of settlers to Indians was overwhelming. The general notion that the American people would eventually settle this country was what was once termed in our history as "manifest destiny." This is still an emotional debate, depending on your ideology. But in reality, our founding history cannot be altered.

Customs and Practices of the Region

When settlers came to this new frontier, they brought their own customs and practices, which soon became the norm in the area. These rituals and methods quickly became routine in many of the pioneer homes and villages that sprang up in the region. Many of these customs were passed on to future generations. Of the natural resources available to the new settlers, wood was plentiful because of bountiful timber in the area.

...and had only to choose the enduring varieties (timber) for permanence. For the zigzag or worm rail fences, the easy splitting chestnut was chosen; for the log cabins, the long slender boles of short leaf yellow pine; for the picket fences of gardens and yards and for covering boards, some easily rived species of oak; for the later development of frame dwellings, pines and oaks or such as yielded to the magic touch of the broadax and adz (probably an axe). The sills of a house were hewn with broadax, and carefully mortised for each corner post, brace and stud in the wall, and each upright timber was firmly pegged into its place at top and bottom... (Smith, 1933)

Cooking was rudimentary by today's standards. The settlers would typically build a freestanding oven structure of stone or brick, complete with a chimney away from the house. A week's supply of food was cooked in one session of baking bread or a whole turkey or ham, or all three at one time, especially during a gathering. Barbecuing and roasting were the most common methods of cooking. A *spider* (we know it as a *Dutch oven*) was a cast-iron pot that stood on three legs. Its lid could be heaped with coals so it could heat or brown the top of biscuits, corn pone, and other foods on an open fireplace. An iron pan or cast-iron skillet was used to fry foods such as bacon, sliced ham, and game steaks. Coals of a fire were used to roast sweet potatoes and cook ashcake (cornbread).

Keeping a fire going was almost a never-ending task, since matches were not commonplace until after the Civil War. Banking ashes over live coals at night was a required duty of someone in the household. This kept the embers radiating overnight and ready for the morning firing of the hearth. Hunters, campers, and long-distance teamsters carried tinderboxes, flint, and steel. Some had a small metal box with spongy remains from decayed trees (the substance was known as *punk*), which when sparked would readily ignite a small fire.

On the plantations, the spring months were for tilling, sowing, planting, and weeding, and the work was never-ending. Later in the season, a strong-armed cradler scythed a swath of ripened grain (wheat, barley, rye, or oats) and would be followed by someone who gathered the fallen grain stalks into bundles. Then came the thrashing day, which entailed hard, intense labor designed to separate the grain kernels from the stems and ready it to be milled.

The days of autumn dedicated to cotton picking, cane grinding, cider making, and corn shucking were held and celebrated in social gatherings. These centered in churches, camp meetings, or plantation gatherings, garnished with a festival-like entertainment. During this time, settling day came on October 1 every year, which was when all open accounts of the barter type were paid. The threshing toll was paid in grain; the miller paid with grain as well, and all other credit was payable in full on settling day.

Corn shucking, also known as a "husking bee" in other parts of the nation, was a time of frenzied work and merriment that broke the monotony of labor and brought all the surrounding neighbors together. It pitted contestants to see who could shuck the first ear of corn or the most corn ears, which entitled the lucky ones to an extra ration of eggnog or hazing by other participants...*the dancing of jigs and singing of old songs interspersed the program of work and amusement.* (Smith, 1933)

Peddler wagons were an occasional, interesting, and unusual event for these remote villages and towns of this western frontier. A peddler with a Conestoga wagon lumbered into the area with a variety of goods and wares: tin cups, pots, pans, plates, buckets, cutlery of all types from knives to axes, ribbon, calico, flannel, and sometimes silk and velvet, liniments, quinine, tonic, and turpentine. Wares were offered for cash or barter in fruits, bacon, horse feed, rags, etc. Sometimes a peddler came with a tinker who sharpened scissors and knives, soldered leaky pans and buckets, and repaired items such as umbrellas and clocks.

Roadwork was completed after most of the crops of the summer were planted, and every able male citizen in a militia district was subject to a *call-up*. A call-up was when all the eroded and washed-out spots and ditches were cleared and repaired. The initial Indian trails and paths were steadily improved even though they were still earthen. Pavement (usually in brick) was reserved for the towns and streets of larger populated areas. This roadwork was later developed into a road tax*, which could be paid by personal labor, or in money, or by the furnishing of certain teams and appliances for road work.* (Smith, 1933)

The fabled country doctor traveled on faintly marked trails and by horseback or buggy to reach his patients in this area. These doctors were not only traveling surgeons; they doubled as dentists, pharmacists, nurses, botanists and anything else required to fulfill the Hippocratic Oath. The doctor (typically male) carried all the tools of the trade:

instruments for operating, materials for bandaging, remedies, sedatives, liniments, and anything used in his pharmacy. On the way to a visitation, he watched for botanicals such as catnip, lobelia, bayberry, gentian, and other plants from which he prepared his tinctures. This was the work of my great-grandfather. From this and other background research and the evidence uncovered about his life, I know he must have been highly dedicated to his profession to have plied his trade in these hard beginnings on this fairly new frontier.

Written matter was scarce, books were few in number, and newspapers were delayed in their arriving. A fireplace provided most of the nightly illumination. Reading was not yet widespread due to time required for chores essential to existence. However, the yearning for knowledge persisted. For the evening hours, candlestick cylinders made from animal fat with twisted cotton yarn in their center became common for lighting a household. The discovery that oil from sperm whales could be mixed with this tallow was the first step forward in improving the technology that allowed nightly studies. ...*The invention of incandescent electric lights by Edison in 1879 marked the beginning of the period which enables night to be transformed into day.* (Smith, 1933)

One has to imagine the schedule of a day in the life of these industrious pioneers. Little reading as done by the general population because of the intense, time-consuming labor that was required to plant and grow food for the family, especially a large one. Therefore, one can imagine that daylight hours were dedicated to labor necessary to sustain oneself and one's family, and nighttime was for getting the sleep one needed to perform that work.

Early Transportation and Mobility

How did my ancestors travel? It is hard to be specific, so I will rely on general historical accounts of early modes of mobility. I surmise that travel in the early years of settlement throughout the area was slow and most likely dependent on existing Native American trails and paths.

Many of the early trails eventually were widened for the incoming wheeled wagon traffic. The goods of those early days were carried by Conestoga wagons with canvas or hide coverings usually drawn by oxen, or mules in teams of two, four, or six to a wagon. Most of the movement of these wagons occurred in a caravan, which provided protection from Indians. Business and pleasure travel was typically on horseback, gig, or in a carriage; for longer distances, a public stagecoach was used. These stagecoaches drew intense curiosity from communities they passed through, as that was the town peoples' contact with the outside world. Word-of-mouth news traveled quickly when the stage arrived from another area.

The federal government in the early 1800s began internal improvements, which would open a trade route between the extreme western settlements of Tennessee and Alabama with the eastern coast of Georgia. Two roads were called the Federal Road. In negotiating a series of treaties with the Creek and Cherokee Indians, the government gained the right to operate roads through Indian lands. The government did not, however, have a major role in building the roads; they relied upon states to do that work. These roads, former Creek and Cherokee trading paths, were in some instances rerouted, and most of them were widened. Evangelists, military veterans, settlers, European travelers, slaves, hunters, and adventurers traveled west on these roads. These movements, coupled with the opening of the territory to land grants and the lottery, speeded up the federal government's plan for moving the Indians beyond the Mississippi River. Additionally, the benefit of these already-blazed trails aided the newcomers in that...*applying for their land grants; the settlers exhibited a strong preference for sites located along major trails. It was a further bonus when the grant contained land formerly occupied and cleared by Indians, known as "Indian old fields." So important were Indian trails that when Georgia became a state, the surveyor general ordered that all land surveyors "insert in their proper places, what runs of water...noted paths or roads" their survey lines crossed. When they constructed their maps of Georgia's early Indian trails, both Goff and Hemperley (early Georgia scholars) relied heavily on original land survey plats that showed these features.* (DeVorsey, 2003)

Later, toward the mid-century, railroads and ferryboats became increasingly prevalent in the area, and the telegraph made its debut, which was to become the main source of long-distance communication with the outside world. The river systems allowed ferry traffic to flow to the more populated areas of Georgia. (Smith, 1933)

Civil War Participation

There is very little documentation of direct Birdsong family involvement in the Civil War from this western Georgia region. In searching the county histories of the area, I found a Troup County history written in 1933 that listed a partial roster of the men of this county who had served in all wars to the time of this writing.

In this document, I found three Birdsong residents of Troup County who were documented as joining the G. V. I., C. S. A. (Georgia Volunteer Infantry – Confederate States of America) early in the war.

G. W. Birdsong, *F – 21, Ga.; July 9, 1861*

John W. Birdsong, *E – 41, Ga.; March 4, 1862; died Harrodsburg, Ky., Nov. 1, 1862.*

Washington F. Birdsong, *F – 21, Ga., July 9, 1861; Provost*

These Birdsongs are not direct relations of Dr. James Christian Birdsong, but were distant cousins living nearby in Troup County when Jimmy was a youngster. (James C. was about fourteen years old when the Civil War began and was living in Carroll County.) This document is likened to our present-day Command Chronology Reports issued as after-action reports, placed in military archives, and unclassified after a number of years.

The units these men joined are described in the history as follows:

The Ben Hill Infantry, Co. F, 21st Reg., G. V. I., C. S. A. This company was named in honor of Benjamin Harvey Hill, Confederate senator.

Troup Light Guards, Co. E, 41st Reg., G. V. I., C. S. A. This company was sometimes called the Curtright Company and was in the Army of Tennessee.

Twenty-First Regiment, G. V. I., C. S. A. This regiment was a part of the Army of Northern Virginia; the muster date was July 9, 1861.

> *1861, July 9. Mustered into service.*
> *1862, March 22. Kernstown, Va.*
> > *June 1. Seven Pines (Fair Oaks).*
> > *June 8. Cross Keys, Va. Strasburg, Va.*
> > *Aug. 8. Cedar Mountain, Va.*
> > *Aug. 30. Second Manassas.*
> > *Sept. 15. Harper's Ferry.*
> > *Dec 13. Fredericksburg, Va.*
> *1863, May 1. Chancellorsville, Va.*
> > *July 1. Gettysburg, Pa.*
> *1865, March 25. Fort Steadman, Va.*
> > *April 9. Appomattox, Va., and surrender.*

Forty-First Regiment, G. V. I., C. S. A. This regiment was a part of General Maney's Brigade of Cheatham's Division of the Army of Tennessee and the Troup Light Guards as Company E of the 41st regiment.

1862, March 4. Mustered into service
        Oct. 6. Murfreesboro, Tenn.
        Oct. 8. Perryville, Ky.
1863, May 16. Baker's Creek, Miss.
        July 4. Vicksburg, Miss. Captured
        July 6. Paroled in exchange.
        Nov. 25. Missionary Ridge, Ga.
1864, Feb 5. Rocky Face, Ga.
        June 18. Kennesaw Mountain, Ga.
        July 31. Jonesboro, Ga. (Atlanta).
1865, Feb. 18. Columbia, S. C.
        March 14. Kinston, N. C.
        April 26. Greensboro, N. C. Surrendered

The roster of the Confederate soldiers, which includes the names of many Troup County citizens that served in widely scattered organizations, is arranged alphabetically in another chapter of this history. It is not complete, but includes all that could be found and identified as Troup County soldiers... (Smith, 1933)

This narrative is but one short expose' of local unit history with timelines. Considering what happened in this war and all of the small and large tragedies, it is overwhelming. Millions of people since the ending of the Civil War have sought to talk about it, re-enact it, watch it choreographed on TV, write book after book about the battles, and delve deeply into the details of most every event from beginning to end. Stop to think about what would have happened had it not occurred: Slavery could have lingered even longer. Would the South have become Balkanized? Usually change occurs slowly, deliberately, and silently, but in the case of this war, it came about suddenly and produced monumental change. It did happen, and though traumatic, the war and its ending brought good things to the nation. Did it happen because our leaders of the time wanted to abolish slavery, or did it happen because of states' rights issues? The debate may go on forever. There is no clear answer, but the people of this nation and my ancestors were clearly affected by the outcome of this catastrophic event. In small ways the effects are revealed in this family history, it's documented past, and through the family stories.

According to Dean John Birdsong's research (Birdsong D. J., Ancestry & Descendants of My Grandparents Dr. James C. Birdsong MD & Mary L. Weaver, 2010), Dr James C. Birdsong's father, "Edlo" (Edmund Lowe), practicing as a veterinarian for the Confederate Army, was captured by Union forces. As a Union prisoner, he was interned on a horse farm in Kentucky intended to supply horses to the Union Army. That account is told in detail in Dean's history. Accordingly, Edlo and his young son Jimmy (James Christian) both worked on the Kentucky horse farm belonging to Abner Eichelburger in the Louisville, Kentucky, area. The speculation is that the rest of the family stayed in the western Georgia in the Carroll County area, west of Atlanta, Georgia, during this period.

War Comes to the Region

The Civil War had a traumatic effect on the towns and
settlements of western Georgia. Although most of the war
up to this time was hard-fought and exhausting, this area of
the country had not yet experienced the brunt of the travails
of war and its destruction. In my research, I found these
heightened conditions (in 1864, a year before the end of the
war) of the western Georgia area described in the following
hard-hitting written history, compiled by John H. Martin
and published soon after the war in 1875.

*1864 - Condition of Columbus the year preceding the
close of the War – Gen. Rosseau's Raid*

*This appears to have been a year of few local incidents
of an exciting character. But it was a year of unusual
business activity in Columbus, and of much feverish
excitement caused by the events of the war. A great many
residents were absent in the army, or in the prosecution of
other public duties, but the city was filled by a transient
population, most working in the factories, foundries, and
other establishments doing work for the Confederate
government or to supply those fabrics usually imported but
now cut off by the state of war.*

Martin writes that the factories of Columbus were
working 24/7 and were a beehive of activity during this
timeline. They were under a military mandate, producing
and assembling many goods and supplies that the
Confederate forces needed in order to prosecute the war.
Two gunboats were constructed and furnished by the
Confederate Naval Works but were out of commission

quickly, one sunk and the other burned by the Union forces. The Chattahoochee River provided an essential waterway for shipping all the way to the Gulf waters. The city had many hospitals, even converting its courthouse, for the sick and wounded soldiers brought in from battlefields to the north and east. Inflation was rampant, raw materials were becoming scarcer, and the currency was in a state of depreciation. *We find the following quotations of prices in April: Flour $350 per barrel; Bacon $4 per pound; Sugar $8 per pound; Coffee $20 per pound; Meal $10 per bushel (Confederate Currency).* (Martin, 1875)

This region didn't record major battles during most of the war. Not much is cataloged in this general area, but further north, a short distance in the Atlanta area, General William Tecumseh Sherman was poised and prepared for his historical sweep through the heart of the South to Savannah, GA.

Columbus was thrown into considerable excitement, in July (1864), by the approach of a large raiding force under command of General Rosseau. This force, supposed to consist of 1500 or 2000 mounted and picked men, came down through north-east Alabama, by way of Talladega, struck the Montgomery & West Point Railroad between Notasulga and Auburn, and thence followed the railroad in the direction of Columbus as far as Opelika (Alabama). The companies organized in Columbus for local defence, consisting of old men, workmen in the shops, foundries, factories, etc., were sent out to oppose their march, and took positions commanding the Crawford and Salem roads, about a mile and half west of the city. This force of undisciplined and poorly armed troops, numbering perhaps six or eight hundred, were under command of Col. DeLagnel in the field, with the supervision of Major Dawson, commandant of the post...The (Union) raiders struck across the country through Chambers County, Alabama, and made their way to Gen. Sherman's lines above Atlanta... (Martin, 1875)

Toward the end of the Civil War on April 16, 1865, Columbus citizens came under attack in what is billed in this manuscript as the *"last battle of the war on this side of the Mississippi river..."* according to reports from the local newspaper, the *Enquirer*, of June 27, 1865. General James H. Wilson played a major role in the coming events.

On Sunday, the 16th of April, the last battle of the war...was fought in Girard, Alabama, opposite this city.

The Confederate troops consisted of two regiments of the Georgia State Line, Waddell's battery, some of the forces of Gens. Buford and Wofford, a small number of the Georgia reserves...numbering in all, perhaps, two thousand men...advance was met by a fire from a small Confederate force near the creek bridge in Girard, and from the battery on the red hill near the upper bridge, and was soon compelled to retire...The order was then given to fire (burn) the bridge, which was quickly carried out, and it was soon wrapped in flames...From two o'clock until dark no attack was made by the Federal troops, though it was evident that they were arriving in considerable numbers and were preparing for the conflict...

In a short time there was a promiscuous rush for the bridge. Friend and foe, horsemen and footmen, artillery wagons and ambulances, were crowded and jammed together in the narrow avenue, which was "dark as Egypt," or "Erebus," for that bridge had no gas fixtures and was never lighted. How it was that many were not crushed to death in this tumultuous transit of the Chattahoochee seems incomprehensible. The Confederates had no reserve forces, except a few squads for guard duty, in the city, and very little resistance was made after the Federals had crossed the bridge. But nearly all the known casualties on the Confederate side nevertheless occurred on this side of the river. (Martin, 1875)

General James H. Wilson was a graduate of West Point in 1860, and was sixth in a class of 41 graduates that year. He was assigned to the Topographical Engineers (Mapping) after graduation. However, circumstance found him in the South during the later years of the war. A favorite of General-in-Chief Ulysses S. Grant, Wilson was supposed to make a diversion for a large force headed for Mobile, Alabama, in the spring of 1865, but he convinced his superiors to allow him a further incursion and independent campaign into Selma, Alabama, one of the Confederacy's major munitions depositories. After securing Selma, he turned his focus toward Columbus, Georgia, *the northernmost navigable point from the Gulf of Mexico and as the place where two railroads converged added to its importance as an industrial center.* (Martin, 1875)

Columbus was also one of the largest textile centers in the southern United States at the time, and was strategically very important for the Union to secure. General Wilson in his after-action reporting was eventually considered only approximately correct, and the actual damage was about half of his original determination. Before leaving the city, his troops destroyed the *Jackson*, nearly ready for sea, and burned 15 steam locomotives, 250 rail cars, the railway bridge and footbridges. In addition, 115,000 bales of cotton, 4 cotton factories, the navy yard, a foundry, an armory, a sword and pistol factory, 3 paper mills, more than 100,000 rounds of artillery ammunition, and other miscellaneous goods were destroyed. Nevertheless, his troops rendered the city captured and in Union hands and prepared to move inward through western Georgia.

Through all the fighting and destruction, neither side knew that the war was drawing to a close…Wilson was unaware of the surrender negotiations in North Carolina between General J. E. Johnston and Union Major General William T. Sherman when he arrived outside Macon on April 19… (Martin, 1875)

Daniel A. Bellware, a member of the Civil War Preservation Trust in Columbus, Georgia in his article "*The Last Battle*" in *Civil War Times*, April 2003, concludes: *The Official Records mention a few skirmishes in the weeks prior to Watie's surrender. But no engagement on the scale of the fight that started in Girard, Alabama, and ended in Columbus, Georgia, occurred after the night of April 16, 1865. Thus, that little-known fight along the Chattahoochee holds the distinction of being the last battle of the Civil War.* (Bellware, 2003)

Martin further highlights the account of General Wilson's departure and "frag orders" (a change to the original operation order) to his units to leave Columbus and make their way toward Macon. He was to move through Talbot County and the burg of Pleasant Hill on what used to be termed as the *Alabama Road,* (now State Highway 36) over the double bridges at the Flint River and on through to Thomaston, Georgia, in Upson County (see 1867 Talbot County Map denoted in Bibliography from the Georgia archives).

The afternoon of the seventeenth I directed Col. Minty to resume his march with his Division on the Thomaston road toward Macon, and to send a detachment forward that night to seize the Double bridges over Flint River. Capt. Van Antwerp, of my staff, accompanied this party. By seven o'clock A. M. the next day he had reached the bridges, fifty miles from Columbus, scattered the party defending them, and took forty prisoners. (Martin, 1875)

Additionally, William H. Davidson in his book, *A Rockaway in Talbot* adds an accounting of General Wilson's men and their passage through the area: *Georgia Highway 36 makes a junction here with the old Alabama Road, to the left, which led to Double Bridges on the Flint River. An historical marker states the bridges crossed the Flint at Owen's Island, one and one quarter miles north of DuBignon's Ferry and two and one half miles northeast of this point... After the fall of Columbus to the Union Troops on April 16, 1865, Confederate Major N. C. Osborn, with 50 Georgia Cavalry Reserves, guarded the bridges. Colonel B. D. Pritchard, after a night march with Fourth Michigan, and Third Ohio Cavalry, overwhelmed the Confederates. Wilson's Raiders followed on April 18 and 19, via Talbotton, Belleview, Pleasant Hill and Thomaston, in nearby Upson County, to rendezvous at Macon.* (Davidson, 1983)

Imagine the state of alarm amongst the citizenry at the presence of Federals as they pressed forward through the city and on into the countryside! This was a devastating blow to the South. Columbus was the center of the great industrial establishments in the region, providing work and support for so many of its citizens and all the cotton that the planters or the surrounding counties had stored here. Its capture and partial destruction ended a long period of prosperity for the area. This was an important regional center of commerce and was the heart of economic prosperity for the close neighboring counties of Carroll, Talbot, Upson, Troup, Harris, Taylor, and Marion, among others.

My ancestors lived in this area, and it is not hard to imagine that they were affected during this time, and most certainly afterword with reconstruction and the extensive rebuilding of the South. My Great-grandmother Mary Lou Weaver's people lived in Talbot County and maintained one of the plantations that sprang up in the early 1800s. In reviewing these historical records, I can imagine what my ancestors must have been thinking and feeling as these events were unfolding.

Not much is known about James Christian Birdsong until after the war. His father Edmund Lowe is enumerated in the 1870 Census as head of household and living in Carroll County (now Carrollton, Georgia). James was about 23 years of age at this time and not listed as living with his mother and father at this time, although most of his siblings were listed in the census.

Emotions of the people in this area during the Civil War and afterward ran high. It likely was pride and loyalty for a way of life more than anything else that spurred the men of the South to join the Confederate Army. When debate about states' rights and secession are set aside, evidence shows that the two armies were more alike than not. Perhaps the most significant characteristic shared by both armies was that the common soldier was largely unaware of (and unprepared for) what he would face in battle.

Imagine the hardships of being in an army that ultimately ran out of most necessities. It was an army that eventually hardened and fought honorably with little or no supplies and little ammunition later in the war. General William Tecumseh Sherman (Union Army) cut a swath through Georgia in the winter months of 1864 from Atlanta to Savannah in his March to the Sea and shut off almost all provisions to the Confederate troops in northern Virginia under General Robert E. Lee. That activity took place in the area northeast of Talbot, Troup, and Upson Counties. Imagine hearing about the campaigns of the Union Army, when the Yankees were coming into the Confederates' own backyard. No doubt the residents felt much uncertainty and despair regarding the invaders.

My research about the Civil War revealed that the war was basically about the types of society that had formed in the North and the South. They were very different ways of life, indeed. The industrial complex concentrated in northern regions, while agriculture bloomed in the southern states.

This was a war of divergent sentiments and opinions that pitted the two societies against one other. Soldiers that fought in this war did not, for the most part, care about sentiment or opinion; they were there because the other side was warring against their way of life. The South fought for states' rights and slavery, but their soldiers were fighting because the invading Yankees were threatening them personally. Most of the Confederates didn't own slaves and had no ideological interest in the reasons for fighting. Nevertheless, they put up a courageous fight throughout all of the campaign and valiantly tried to repel the invaders.

This is the nature of the Southern male; many of these men have an innate warrior psyche. They consistently fill the ranks of our military with an abundance of volunteers. More often than not, career military men are from the Southern states. They can be counted on when the chips are down and all hell is breaking loose. They have long been steadfast and loyal in the ranks of our nation's military organizations throughout our country's history.

I witnessed this strength and loyalty of Southerners during my two tours in Vietnam, and am not the only one who shares this sentiment. A U.S. Marine Corps company commander, a veteran of the TET offensive of 1968 (Northern I Corps, Vietnam), described to me those same basic characteristics about the loyal and brave Southerners he led during battle. Another platoon commander I know, who was at Khe Sanh, expressed the same sentiments about Southern men and Hispanics. He told me that they could be faithfully counted upon to bravely handle whatever faced them, even if it meant certain death.

Chapter 2 ~ My Grandfather's Georgia

Talbot County, Georgia

My grandfather, Herbert Monroe "Hiram" Birdsong, was born in western Georgia in the town of Pleasant Hill in Talbot County. Talbot is west of Upson County and southeast of Troup County by about 25 to 30 miles. The city of Talbotton is the county seat. This area is along the same Alabama Road described earlier, which General J. H. Wilson's Army traveled in April of 1865, over the Double Bridges of the Flint River on their way to Macon. They traveled by the homestead plantation of the Weavers, my great-grandfather's future wife Mary Lou and her family. The Alabama Road south of their place is named on the archive map of Talbot County circa 1867. This area is close to a couple of present-day landmarks. The first is associated with Franklin D. Roosevelt, the thirty-second U.S. President (from 1933 to 1945), who maintained a small vacation home close to Warm Springs, Georgia. Roosevelt's cottage is about 10 to 12 miles northwest of the area where Herbert M. Birdsong was born. Roosevelt came to this area while he was running for president in 1924, to find therapeutic relief from polio in the naturally heated spring waters of Pine Mountain, Georgia. In 1932 he built a small vacation home on this mountain, which became known as the "little White House."

The second notable landmark in this area is Fort Benning, Georgia, located approximately 30 miles to the southwest of Talbot County near Columbus, Georgia. Fort

Benning is named for Brigadier General Henry L. Benning, a Confederate army general and a native of Columbus. It is where all airborne paratroopers are trained in today's army. With these current geographical landmarks established, let us reference the following 1867 map:

The 1867 Talbot County map source:
http://content.sos.state.ga.us/cdm4/county_maps/cmf0321.j
pg (Georgia, Talbot County Map 1867, 1867)

The importance of this map is noted in the book, *A Rockaway in Talbot: Travels in an old Georgia County,* by William H. Davidson, an area historian. A *rockaway* was a horse-drawn buggy. This book validates the purchase of land by Dr. James Christian Birdsong (Herbert Monroe Birdsong's father) near the place where my grandfather was born. Here is a quote from page 510 of Vol. II of this book:

DR. J.C. BIRDSONG PLACE _– *About one mile east of Evans Chapel United Methodist Church on Valley Road, the Dr. James C. Birdsong farmhouse and a small cottage are on the north side of the road. They are at the northwest corner as a short, unpaved road makes a turn from the Valley Road to the Benjamin Burks Kendrick plantation.*

On the northwest corner, opposite the Birdsong houses, is the old James M. Weaver (Dr. J.C.'s father-in-law) plantation house site.

Dr. Birdsong attended the public sale of real estate of George B. Elder, deceased, of Talbot County, on the first Tuesday in November, 1881. Thomas L. Patrick was the administrator of the Elder estate and knocked off the 112 ½ acres of Land Lot No. 157, in the 1ˢᵗ Land District, Valley G. M. D. 902, on Dr. Birdsong's highest bid of $453.00.

The legal description of the land is somewhat typical of the times:...commencing at the southeast corner of said lot and running north fifteen chains to a chestnut tree, thence west fifteen chains to a chestnut stump, thence north fifteen chains to a Black Gum tree, thence west thirty chains to a Popular tree, thence south thirty chains to a Post Oak stump, thence east forty-four chains to a the place of beginning.

Dr. Birdsong's farm was expanded with the purchase from C. F. Jordan, of Talbot County, of the north half of

Land Lot No. 158, 1st Land District, and adjoining No. 157 *on the west. The line dividing the lot ran due east and west.* *Consideration was $925.00, and the deed is dated May 10,* *1897.*

The main Birdsong house was built of lumber from the *Weaver plantation house, demolished by the cyclone of* *May 1, 1875. The smaller cottage was built after 1900.*

Mary Lou Weaver, daughter of James M. and Jane *Amanda Weaver, was married to Dr. James C. Birdsong.* *They were the parents of eleven children. Mrs. Birdsong* *died at her home April 13, 1896 and her burial was in* *Valley Grove Baptist Church Cemetery at Tax.* (Davidson, 1983)

Closer inspection of the 1867 Talbot County map denotes 1st Land District and Land Lot Numbers 157 and 158 in the northeastern section of the map. Take note on the legend that the 1867 map is scaled 90 chains per inch. The New Webster's Dictionary describes a chain as: *surv. A* *measuring instrument, consisting of 100 links, and having a* *total length of 66 feet.*

It is important to expand on this measuring methodology, which explains the foundation for topographical mapping and survey technologies. Invented by clergyman Edmund Gunter, this chain implement was used to accurately measure acreage and lots within an acre. Gunter was of Welsh descent and studied the use of instruments of math with the sole purpose of making mathematical practitioners' work easier, including those who were the land surveyors and navigators aboard seafaring ships. This chain, it seems, has been used consistently throughout the early movement of people opening new frontiers and regions throughout America. It has been used to map territories and lay out cities, townships, granges, and railroads.

By 1785, only Gunter's 66-foot chain was allowed for land surveying work. When I think of listening to my great-uncles, the Giesicks, who were Kansas wheat farmers on my grandmother's side, I remember them telling my father and me that a section of ground is one mile by one mile. There are four quarters of ground in that section of ground (each quarter consisting of 160 acres), or 640 acres in that one square mile. Later I learned an acre of land is equal to 10 square chains. A square mile is equal to 640 acres or 6,400 square chains (80 chains on each side, 80 x 80 = 6,400). If you drive through the dirt farm road grids of the central United States, especially in Kansas, Oklahoma, Colorado, and Nebraska, you will experience this layout of *sections* in mile after mile of farm ground. From one road to the next is usually one mile. This is the basis for sections, quarters, acres, and chains, the grid layout of our nation's farmland.

Using today's technology in topographies, let us now focus on the USGS Manchester, Georgia, Quadrangle 7.5 Minute Series (Topographical) Map, photo-revised 1985, and continue the discussion of the Dr. J. C. Birdsong family homestead location. The first illustrated partial map is the top-right section of the whole map; the second illustration is the bottom-right portion of the map and its datum. Notice the first map and the red circle above Chalybeate Springs Road (also known as Valley Road in earlier times). This area indicates the location of Dr. James Birdsong's purchase of Land Lot No. 157 and 158, identified on the previous Talbot County Map of 1867 from the Georgia Archives. The second map is used to establish the datum of this area. The small squares (dark, open rectangles) inside the red circled area symbolize buildings, both inhabited and uninhabited. The parallel dotted lines aimed in a northerly azimuth, adjacent to the building symbols, indicate an unimproved or private road off the main Chalybeate Springs road highlighted in yellow. The approximate latitude and longitude of this property is 32° 49' 30" N and 84° 31' 15" W.

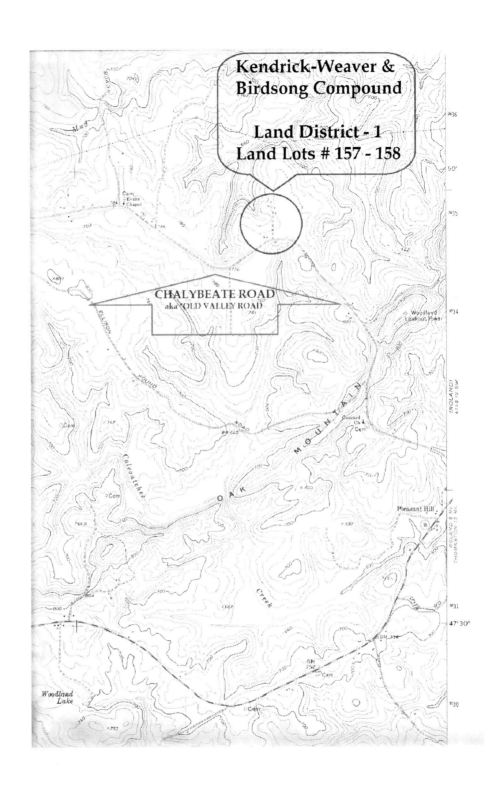

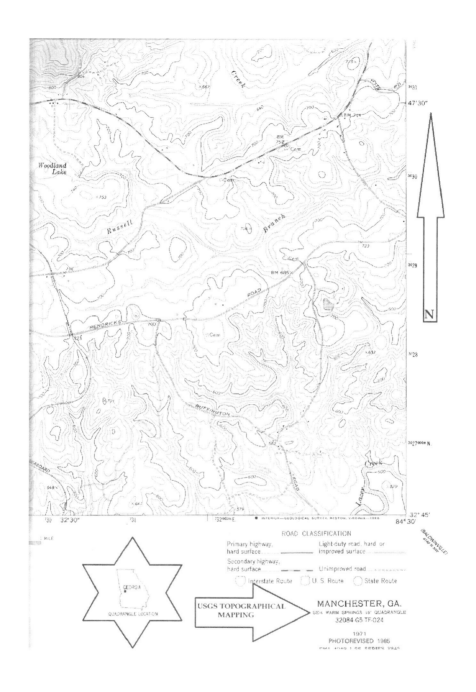

USGS Topographical of Manchester, Georgia

This gives an overview of the geographies of the area where Herbert "Hiram" Monroe Birdsong's father and mother settled, labored, and raised a large family of which Hiram was their youngest. (Technically, E. B. Birdsong, born to Sallie, the second wife, was James C. Birdsong's youngest.) To understand the makeup of my Grandfather Hiram's character and lay the foundation for his sense of family, despite him being orphaned at a young age, I think it fitting to quote from Dr. James Christian Birdsong's obituary in the Talbotton, Georgia, newspaper of July 9, 1902:

No man ever studied his profession harder, or worked it more faithfully than did he. His territory covered a large mountainous area that required much labor to serve, but he responded to the call of the rich and poor, white and black, regardless of compensation until he wore his lite out in the service of his countrymen. As I go into the homes I hear them speak in the highest terms of Dr. Birdsong. They say he was so kind, faithful, good and patient. "Just pay me what you can, and when you can", was his rate, and it kept him poor... (Birdsong D. J., Ancestry & Descendants of My Grandparents Dr. James C. Birdsong MD & Mary L. Weaver, 2010)

Although character is mostly learned, genes and fate contributes to a person's being. From what I gather about my grandfather, he was a good, decent, and wholesome man, which doesn't happen without some help—perhaps from the blessings and design of a higher being. I cannot explain how he learned these qualities, but I have heard too many stories from others to discount them. He was my grandfather and a good one at that. I liked very much the little I remember of him, and I have been mesmerized hearing the many stories about him. Why else would I feel compelled to write about him and my grandmother?

Pleasant Hill, Georgia, and the Valley

Grandfather Herbert's father, Dr. James Christian Birdsong, raised a family of 12 children in the area where his wife Mary Lou Weaver's family settled. Some of them still remain in that area.

Pasture lands on each side of the road now make a setting for interesting gneiss rock formations. An outcropping called by the author 'Little Stone Mountain,' is on the north near the old Dr. James C. Birdsong house. In the pasture, along the south side of the road, is a curious rolling stone… House and guest cottage are in a grove of old oaks and cedars. Some English boxwood from the nearby site of the James M. Weaver (his mother's father) antebellum mansion borders a walk…The Birdsong place corners at an unpaved road turning left and ending at the Benjamin Burks Kendrick plantation, where his descendants still live… (Davidson, 1983)

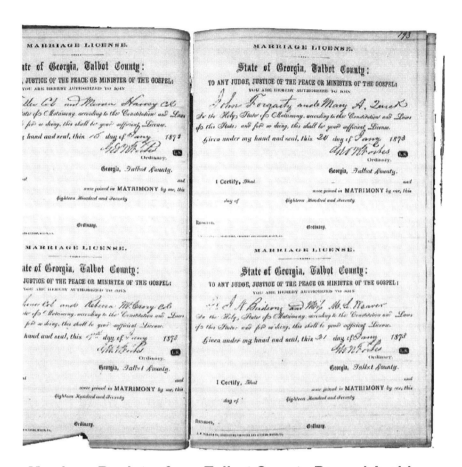

**Marriage Register from Talbot County Record Archive
(Georgia, Marriage Licenses, 1897) Record of Dr. J. C. and
Mary Lou Birdsong's Marriage**

After the Civil War, railroads expanded and brought with them an increase in commerce and population. As these communities prospered and grew, Dr. James Christian Birdsong began his practice in the Pleasant Hill–Woodland area. One can only imagine what it was like covering the area as a country doctor on horseback and buggy. In his book, *There Was a Land: A Story of Talbot County, Georgia, and Its people (*Columbus, Ga., 1971), by Robert

H. Jordan, he describes in short a snapshot of the local society of the northern area of Talbot County.

These families were the ones who supported the churches and schools and were instrumental in creating a very interesting and thriving community. Most of those who moved were farmers but there were sawmill operators, carpenters, blacksmiths, cabinet makers and many other trades. Among those were Bob Trussell, blacksmith; Will O'Neal, blacksmith and miller; H. T. Woodall, farmer; J. C. Pye, merchant, cotton buyer, gin operator; Dan Owen, farmer, grist mill and gin; W. A. Willis, postmaster; Tom Ferguson, rural letter carrier; Seab Woodall: Merchant; Jim and H. P. McDaniel: L. P. Sewell: Madison Mills. Henry F. Ferguson, merchant; Dr. J. C. Birdsong, who covered the area on buggy and on horseback;...the post office was opened on March 5, 1907 in the store now owned by E. B. Birdsong (youngest son of Dr. Birdsong)... Also in 1907 the Matthews gin began to operate...The first passenger train of the A. B. & A. Railroad made its first run on the first Sunday in March, 1907. Many people for miles around came to the depot on this afternoon to see this great "iron horse" and celebrate the event. (Jordon, 1971)

The population of the area at that time was slowly growing. In the *First Lessons in Georgia History* by Lawton B. Evans, the author lists the person for whom each county was named, when it was founded, and the population in 1910. Note that Talbot County was founded in 1827 and had a population of 11,696 in the year 1910 when this history was published. The surrounding counties of Troup and Upson had larger populations. Troup County had the largest number in the immediate area at 26,228, followed by Upson with 12,757. The city of Thomaston, the Upson County Seat, was a large center of activity during this period. Columbus, Georgia, was and is the largest and major population center located on the main regional waterway, the Chattahoochee River. It is approximately 30 miles to the southwest of Talbotton, Geogia. Not shown is Muscogee County, named after the Muscogee Indians. Columbus, the county seat, was founded in 1826 and in 1910 had the largest population: 36,227. (Evans, 1913)

Name.	For Whom.	County Seat.	Laid out.	Population.
Newton........	Sergeant John Newton..	Covington....	1821	18,449
Oconee........	Oconee River........	Watkinsville..	1875	11,104
Oglethorpe....	Gen. Jas. E. Oglethorpe.	Lexington....	1793	18,680
Paulding......	John Paulding......	Dallas........	1832	14,124
Pickens.......	Gen. Andrew Pickens ..	Jasper........	1853	9,041
Pierce.........	Franklin Pierce	Blackshear...	1857	10,749
Pike..........	Zebulon M. Pike ...	Zebulon.....	1822	19,495
Polk..........	Jas. K. Polk.........	Cedartown...	1851	20,203
Pulaski.......	Count Pulaski........	Hawkinsville.	1808	22,835
Putnam.......	Israel Putnam.......	Eatonton.....	1807	13,876
Quitman.......	Gen. John A. Quitman.	Georgetown ..	1858	4,594
Rabun........	Gov. Wm. Rabun...	Clayton.....	1819	5,562
Randolph.....	John Randolph.	Cuthbert.....	1828	18,841
Richmond.....	Duke of Richmond.....	Augusta......	1777	58,886
Rockdale......	"Rockdale Church" .	Conyers	1870	8,916
Schley........	Gov. Wm. Schley.....	Ellaville......	1857	5,213
Screven......	Gen. Jas. Screven.	Sylvania	1793	20,202
Spalding	Hon. Thos. Spalding ...	Griffin.......	1851	19,741
Stephens......	Gov. Alex. H. Stephens.	Toccoa.......	1905	9,728
Stewart.......	Gen. Dan'l Stewart....	Lumpkin.....	1830	13,437
Sumter.......	Gen. Thos. Sumter ..	Americus.....	1831	29,092
Talbot........	Gov. Matthew Talbot.	Talbotton....	1827	11,696
Taliaferro	Col. Benj. Taliaferro...	Crawfordville	1825	8,766
Tattnal........	Josiah Tattnal.........	Reidsville....	1801	18,569
Taylor........	Zach. Taylor.........	Butler.......	1852	10,839
Telfair........	Gov. Edward Telfair.	McRae......	1807	13,288
Terrell........	Dr. Wm. Terrell	Dawson......	1856	22,003
Thomas.......	Gen. Jett Thomas.....	Thomasville..	1825	29,071
Tift...........	Nelson Tift.........	Tifton......	1905	11,487
Toombs.......	Gen. Robert Toombs..	Lyons.......	1905	11,206
Towns........	Gov. Geo. N. Towns...	Hiwassee....	1856	3,932
Troup.........	Gov. Geo. M. Troup ..	Lagrange.....	1826	26,228
Turner........	Henry G. Turner.......	Ashburn.....	1905	10,075
Twiggs........	Gen. John Twiggs.....	Jeffersonville.	1809	10,736
Union.........	Union.............	Blairsville....	1832	6,918
Upson.........	Stephen Upson........	Thomaston...	1824	12,757
Walker........	Maj. Freeman Walker.	La Fayette...	1833	18,692

**Population and Names of Counties from Evans book
(Evans, 1913)**

Herbert Monroe Birdsong was born on November 11, 1895, in Pleasant Hill, Talbot County, Georgia, most likely in the home of his father and mother. Not much is known about his childhood, as his mother Mary Lou died when he was a small boy and he had few recollections of her. Very little is known about his past; he rarely talked about it, other than mentioning that he was raised for a short time by relatives and was surrounded by some sisters and brothers. There are no stories about his mother from any surviving member of the family. It is known that he bonded with and followed his older brother James Christian Jr. almost everywhere. After their mother's death, their father married his late wife Mary Lou's sister, Sallie Harris (Weaver) Olive, in 1897. They had a son in 1898 that they named Earnest Boykin. Sallie Harris Birdsong, J. C. Birdsong's second wife, is buried in Tax Cemetery, above Woodland, Georgia. Sallie was born on August 26, 1863, and passed on September 12, 1924. Their only son, Earnest Boykin Birdsong, became a newspaper columnist and merchant in the small- town of Woodland, Georgia.

Mrs. Sallie Weaver Olive was married to Dr. Birdsong. They were the parents of a son, E. B. Birdsong, a merchant of Woodland. He was popular as a humorous columnist for the Talbotton New Era (local newspaper). Dr. Birdsong died in 1909. [This must be typographical error in the book; the correct date is 1902.]

E. B. Birdsong married Lina Holmes. Their son, E. B. Birdsong, Jr., and family, live in Woodland... (Davidson, 1983)

Marriage License from Archive (Dr. J. C Birdsong.'s second marriage) (Georgia, Marriage Licenses, 1897)

The 1900 Census established the Birdsong family in the Valley District #902 in Talbot County on June 6, 1900. Herbert M. is listed as part of the Birdsong family, with stepmother Sallie H. (Harris) noted as the wife of his father, Dr. James C. Birdsong. The older children, Cornelia, Walter Weaver, and James Edmund had established themselves outside of the home. The number of years of Dr. James C. and Sallie's marriage is noted at three; therefore Grandfather Hiram, the youngest child, was part of this household up to the time of the census.

		Name	Relationship	Color	Sex	Month born	Year born	Age	Marital status	Yrs married	No. children	Place of birth	Father birthplace	Mother birthplace	Occupation	Education
25 9		Birdsong, James C.	H	W	M	July 47	52	m	34			GA	GA	GA	Doctor & Farmer	
		—, Sallie H.	W	W	F	Aug 18	36	m	3	3	3	"	"		Farmer / At school	5
		Alice, Samuel	son	W	M	Aug 15		S								5
		—, Young Allen	son	W	M	Feb 11		S								
		Birdsong Ernest B.	son	W	M	May 2		S								
		—, Janie L.	dau	W	F	July 22		S								
		—, Lyda	dau	W	F	Feb 83	17	S							at sch.	5
		—, Columbus B.	son	W	M	15		S							"	5
		—, Charley	son	W	M	13		S							"	5
		—, Carrie L.	dau	W	F	11		S							"	5
		—, Sallie W.	dau	W	F	June 8		S							"	5
		—, James C.	son	W	M	Feb 7		S								
		—, Herbert	son	W	M	May 5		S								

1900 Census – United States (Recreated from Microfilm Roll # 1,240,222 – Talbot County, Georgia, by D. J. Birdsong)

From reading Dean J. Birdsong's research and perusing the Talbot Court of Ordinary proceedings, it is hard to visualize the complete picture of what happened to the children after the death of Dr. James Birdsong. It is clear, however, that Dr. and Mary Lou Birdsong's children were placed under the guardianship of the court by their stepmother Sallie Harris (Weaver) Birdsong.

Closer examination of those proceedings show that on November 21, 1902, E. T. Smith was assigned guardianship and given $1000 to maintain, clothe, and educate the orphans of James C. Birdsong (Carrie L., Sallie W., James C., and Herbert M.) by and according to the laws of the state of Georgia. The other older children, Charlie, Columbus "Lum" Bryant, and Lydia were assigned to the older daughter, Janie Amanda, who had married Sidney Marvin Alsobrooke. The Alsobrookes became guardians of the older siblings until they came of legal age. Dean John Birdsong provided these documents from his collection of documents notated in his latest book. (Birdsong D. J., Ancestry & Descendants of My Grandparents Dr. James C. Birdsong MD & Mary L. Weaver, 2010)

Family Group Chart

Dr. James Christian and Mary Lou Birdsong Family, Pleasant Hill, Talbot County, Georgia 1800-1900s. The Initial research by Dean J. Birdsong. Formatted and updated by Grady T. Birdsong.

Husband	Dr. James Christian Birdsong	
Birth	Jul. 10, 1847	Talbot County, Georgia, USA
Marriage	Jan. 21, 1873	
Death	May 27, 1902	Talbot County, Georgia, USA
Burial		
Other Wife	Sallie Harris Birdsong [Weaver (sister of Mary Lou Weaver - married 1897)]	
Parents	Edmund Lowe Birdsong and Sarah Birdsong [Wicks]	

Wife	Mary Lou Birdsong [Weaver]	
Birth	Jun. 18, 1852	Talbot County, Georgia, USA
Death	Apr. 8, 1896	Talbot County, Georgia, USA
Burial		
Other Husbands		
Parents	James M Weaver and Jane Amanda Weaver [Harris]	

Children		

1	Infant Birdsong	
Gender	Male	
Birth	May 21, 1874	Talbot County, Georgia, USA
Wife		
Marriage		
Death	May 21, 1874	Talbot County, Georgia, USA
Burial		

2	Cornelia Kendrick [Birdsong]	
Gender	Female	
Birth	Aug. 8, 1875	Talbot County, Georgia, USA
Husband	Henry Binns Kendrick	
Marriage	Dec. 23, 1896	Talbot County, Georgia, USA
Death	Jun. 11, 1961	Talbot County, Georgia, USA
Burial		Talbot County, Georgia, USA

3	Janie Amanda Alsobrooks [Birdsong]	
Gender	Female	
Birth	Jul. 8, 1877	Talbot County, Georgia, USA
Husband	**Sidney Marvin Sr. Alsobrooks**	
Marriage	Oct. 9, 1900	Talbot County, Georgia, USA
Death	Jun. 1, 1946	Talbot County, Georgia, USA
Burial		

4	Walter Weaver Birdsong	
Gender	Male	
Birth	Jan. 26, 1879	Talbot County, Georgia, USA
Wife		
Marriage		
Death		
Burial		

5	James Edmund Birdsong	
Gender	Male	
Birth	Nov. 23, 1880	Talbot County, Georgia, USA
Wife		
Marriage		
Death	1949	Talbot County, Georgia, USA
Burial		Valley Grove, Talbot County, Georgia, USA

6	Lydia Davis [Birdsong]	
Gender	Female	
Birth	Feb. 28, 1883	Talbot County, Georgia, USA
Husband	**Arthur Worrell Sr. Davis**	
Marriage	Jan. 21, 1903	Talbot County, Georgia, USA
Death	Feb. 26, 1950	Columbus, Muscogee County, Georgia, USA
Burial		Parkhill Cemetery, Columbus, GA

7	Columbus Bryant "Lum" Birdsong	
Gender	Male	
Birth	Dec. 12, 1884	Talbot County, Georgia, USA
Wife		
Marriage		
Death	Mar. 13, 1948	Talbot County, Georgia, USA
Burial		Centerville Cemetery, Talbot County, Georgia, USA

8	Charles "Charley" Birdsong	
Gender	Male	
Birth	Jan. 2, 1887	Talbot County, Georgia, USA
Wife		
Marriage		
Death		Birmingham, AL
Burial		

9	Carrie Lou Davis [Birdsong]	
Gender	Female	
Birth	May 5, 1889	Talbot County, Georgia, USA
Husband	Clarence E. Davis	
Marriage	Jan. 6, 1907	Talbot County, Georgia, USA
Death	Oct. 10, 1941	Prattsburgh, Talbot County, Georgia, USA
Burial		Cornith ME Cemetery, Prattsburgh, GA

10	Sallie Weeks Morris [Birdsong]	
Gender	Female	
Birth	Jun. 10, 1891	Talbot County, Georgia, USA
Husband	Arthur Ross Morris	
Marriage	Aug. 2, 1908	Talbot County, Georgia, USA
Death	Jun. 2, 1963	Talbot County, Georgia, USA
Burial		Valley Grove Cemetery, Talbot County, Georgia, USA

11	James Christian Birdsong, Jr.	
Gender	Male	
Birth	Oct. 30, 1893	Talbot County, Georgia, USA
Wife	Opal Maurine Birdsong [Neal]	
Marriage	Feb. 1918	McCracken, Kansas
Death	Aug. 25, 1975	Marquette, McPherson, KS
Burial		Marquette Cemetery

12	Herbert Monroe Birdsong	
Gender	Male	
Birth	Nov. 11, 1895	Talbot County, Georgia, USA
Wife	Martha Birdsong [Giesick]	
Marriage	Sep. 20, 1922	Ellsworth, KS
Death	Jan. 25, 1950	Garden City, Kansas
Burial		Hoisington Kansas

13	Ernest Boykin Birdsong (by Sallie Harris Weaver {Olive} - 2nd Wife)	
Gender	Male	
Birth	May 4, 1898	Talbot County, Georgia, USA
Wife	Lina Livingston Birdsong [Holmes]	
Marriage	1918	
Death	Mar. 26, 1972	Woodland, Talbot County, Georgia, USA
Burial		

Chapter 3 ~ The Journey to Kansas

How did Grandfather Herbert M. Birdsong make his way to Kansas? When? Why?

Leaving Georgia

My father told us numerous times how Grandfather Herbert began his journey to Kansas. This is how my dad tells the story: Herbert and his older brother, James (also known as "Jim") decided to leave Georgia because they heard that good money could be made in the wheat fields of Kansas. Hence, one day they went to the local river (it isn't clear which river or creek), which was either flooding or swollen. Because Grandfather couldn't swim, Jim, who was older, crossed the river and yelled to Herbert to go back, saying he would send for him once he got established. (Birdsong D. J., Disscussion of Family, 2010)

In the area of Pleasant Hill, Georgia, the closest body of running water near the late Dr. Birdsong's land is known now as Coleoatchee Creek (also called Celeoth Creek by the locals). The closest larger river is the Flint River, about six or seven miles to the east, in the direction of the town of Thomaston, Georgia. Celeoth Creek is not deep or wide, but it is conceivable that it could flood to larger proportions if conditions were right. It is hard to speculate which body of water is referred to in this oral family story. I believe there is some element of fact to this version because it has been consistently told over the years and was originally told to the family by my grandfather and his brother, Jim.

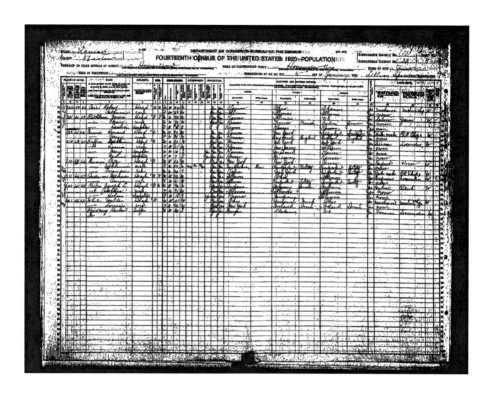

**Fourteenth Census of the United States, 1920 –
Population (Government U. S., Fourteenth Census, 1920)**

**State: Kansas, County: Barton, Township: Homestead,
Place: Hoisington**

Enumerated: 5 January 1920; signed by Lillian Spencer

A Railroad Career Begins

The Census of 1920, upon closer inspection, shows Herbert
Birdsong living in Hoisington, Kansas, as a lodger at the age
of 24, being able to read and write and enumerated as *"w,"* a
wage earner. It shows he is from Georgia, and also specifies
that he is a locomotive fireman on the railroad and is living

(boarding) with Walter and Louise White (ages 41 and 38, respectively) on 201 E. Fourth Street.

Walter White is listed as a machinist. It is likely that the only place a machinist would have been employed during those times was at the roundhouse of the Missouri Pacific (MoPac) Railroad, close to the tracks of the station house (depot) in Hoisington, Kansas. More than likely, Herbert and Walter were friends or acquaintances because of their jobs. The roundhouse was a facility for maintenance on the locomotives and other over-the-rail equipment. The "round" in the term meant that locomotives and or any rolling stock brought into the facility could be positioned in direction up to 170 degrees on a gigantic, semi-round mechanical table of track and placed into the working pit or stalls for overhaul or repair. This facility was halfway between the Missouri Pacific's major hubs (terminals) of Sedalia, Missouri, near Kansas City and out to the far west in Pueblo, Colorado. (Government U. S., Fourteenth Census, 1920)

When searching for details about the Hoisington roundhouse, I came across the Kansas Trails website (Kansas Trails Web Site, Peggy Thompson) and a biographical history of Barton County, Kansas. With the permission of the Kansas Trails webmaster, I am submitting the following posted writing, which was written at the time when the roundhouse was built and started operating in the early 1900s:

Hoisington is the freight and passenger division on the Missouri Pacific railroad and the company operates at this point the largest shops between Sedalia (Missouri) and

Pueblo (Colorado), and next to the Sedalia shops, are the largest owned by this company on its entire system. The pay roll of the railroad men in Hoisington adds greatly to the prosperity of the city and makes it not alone dependent on the farmers in the surrounding country for trade.

September 28, 1910, work was begun on the first building that makes up the large number composing the Missouri Pacific shops. This building is the roundhouse and has a concrete foundation with fifteen 63-foot engine pits. It is a brick building with the most modern apparatus and appliances. Two sides of the structure are composed of glass which allows plenty of light to filter in. It contains 2,000 yards of concrete, has a turntable with a diameter of seventy-five feet, a 100,000-gallon capacity hot well for the purpose of washing boilers, etc.

The coal chute has a capacity of 500 tons of coal and is the type made by the Robinson & Schafer Co. It has elevators with a capacity for lifting 125 tons of coal per hour and a storage capacity for fifteen tons of sand. Green sand is made ready for use after it has been lifted by a Holeman elevator system to the top of the chute where it is dried by a steam drying apparatus. From the dryer it is conducted through chutes to the storage bins from where it is supplied to the engines as needed. This system almost entirely eliminates hand work and results in a high-class product. Near the coal chutes are found two 100,000 -gallon water tanks that afford an endless supply of good water. The water is forced into the tanks by modern pumping systems and their close proximity to the coal chutes makes it possible for an engine to be supplied with coal, water and sand in the shortest possible time.

The cinder pit on which work was begun October 24, 1910, is 225 feet in length with a depressed track which allows the work of cleaning the fire box of an engine to be done quickly and thoroughly.

The blacksmith and machine buildings are large and equipped with all the latest labor saving machinery and are capable of turning out a great amount of work in the shortest possible time and when in full operation will give employment to a large number of men.

The system by which water is supplied to all parts of the different buildings is composed of three wells near the powerhouse - powerful pumps that force water into the pipe lines that conduct it to all parts of the works. The reservoir for the reserve of water has a capacity of 100,000 gallons.

On the grounds are found a number of other buildings which include the offices of the different heads of departments and when the shops are working at full capacity, it is expected that a force of 1,600 men will be required. The total cost of the plant is about $1,000,000. All the buildings are amply protected against fire by the latest and most approved methods.

The Missouri Pacific shop is an establishment of which the people of Barton County are justly proud and it is a big thing for the town of Hoisington from a business standpoint. (Kansas Trails Web Site, Peggy Thompson)

This is an excellent technical description of the roundhouse capabilities in this period. It was considered a state-of-the-art railroad machine shop and roundhouse, which brought work and additional industry to the area. My father told me that MoPac sponsored an apprentice program in conjunction with the roundhouse. He reminisced that MoPac paid men approximately $125 per month to work and study as apprentice machinists. At the time, the railroads were major players in the transport of wheat and grain to market in these wheat-state regions. Passenger service was a secondary market for these rural areas. Grandfather Herbert was about to begin his career at this major junction of early 1900s technology, which was during the beginning of the end of the industrial revolution.

I was fortunate to make a writing acquaintance through Hoisington native Robert Glynn. His friend, Joseph E. Johnson, Hoisington native, is an American Legion Historian, Department of Kansas, and a WWII veteran. Johnson, who now lives in Cawker City, Kansas, describes the roundhouse he knew in the 1940s: *It was for repair work, servicing and testing. Every steam locomotive that arrived in Hoisington had to be filled with water and coal, the sand domes filled with sand (for traction when starting or going up a grade), greased and [given] minor repairs if needed. Many times the locomotive would be taken off line and another one would be ready to pull the train to save time...*

Hoisington is half way between Kansas City and Pueblo, Colorado, which is as far as a steam locomotive could go without being serviced. The MoPac had three shops where locomotives were re-built: Little Rock, Arkansas; Sedalia, Missouri; and Hoisington, Kansas. I don't remember how often the steam locomotives had to be rebuilt, but this was done in the "back shop," as it was called. A locomotive was torn down completely; everything was stripped off, even the insulation. All that was left was the bare boiler and the cab. Then it was put back together with all worn parts replaced or machined to fit. Then the painter would spray a shiny coat of black paint on it and re-letter with white paint. I can easily see why the railroads did away with steam. It must have cost a lot to maintain the steam locomotives. (Johnson J. E., 2010)

My grandfather was for a time a locomotive fireman. Railroad Retirement Board personnel records notate that my grandfather was an engine watchman in the Colorado Division (McCracken, KS) from December 1913 until August 23, 1916. On August 25, 1916, he was promoted to fireman and remained in that occupational duty until July 13, 1926, when he became an engineer. The exact date he moved to Hoisington from McCracken and resumed fireman status in the Kansas Division is unknown. Close study of Railroad Retirement Board records indicates that he went to Hoisington sometime in the latter part of 1916. My grandfather's Employee Personnel Record shows that he was employed in McCracken, Kansas, Colorado Division, as early as December 1913. (Pay records were not available, but his presence was established, check-marked, and acknowledged by MoPac and Railroad Retirement Board personnel records.) (Board, 2011)

To answer the question of how Grandfather made his way to Kansas, I have ascertained that before his arrival in McCracken, Grandfather traveled by riding the rails, hitchhiking, and/or walking (or a combination of these) to

Kansas from Georgia, sometime between July 1912 and late 1913, a span of approximately one and half years. Talbot County Court records cite guardianship of him and his brother James on July 1, 1912, which places both in Georgia at that time.

The duties of a fireman varied, with each fireman starting at the bottom rung of a fireman's hierarchal ladder of railroad jobs. From researching railroad history and listening to family stories, I learned that "paying one's dues" was required through completing certain jobs and tasks. Gathering supplies, engine-wiper duties, emptying and cleaning ash pans, filling lubricators and oilcans, checking hot boxes (axle bearings on the box and freight car wheels), keeping engine fittings wiped clean, filling sand boxes, and sundry other drudgery-type jobs were required to keep the rolling stock moving on the rails. If a junior fireman performed these jobs to his superior's satisfaction, he could expect to be promoted up the various rungs of the job ladder to become a regular fireman.

The regular fireman's job was to shovel coal into the firebox on the locomotive's boiler to make sure it maintained good steam pressure. A fireman also served as the co-pilot in that he was not only a pair of hands, but a second set of eyes to observe signaling devices, curves, and grade changes that might require additional pressure (he would shovel more coal) and address the nuances that might arise in the course of a run or trip. My father often spoke of his father's best friend and mentor, an older man named Jake Crane. Jake was one of the senior engineers for the Missouri Pacific railroad based in Hoisington. Jake told my dad that

Grandfather Herbert *"was a good fireman"* and that he was *"the best we had!"* Jake told my father at Grandfather Herbert's funeral that *"He was a hard worker and hard to work for, and you had to do your job when you worked for him."* I also heard many stories about Jake, and came to know that he was a legend among the men of the MoPac around Hoisington.

Herbert "Hiram" Birdsong's Fireman's Shovel.
SturdE-SteelB **Patent, U.S. November 4, 1919 and January 20, 1925. Inscribed M.P.R.R. ~ W.S.&T. CO (Birdsong W. J., Photograph of Fireman Shovel MPRR {Missouri Pacific Rail Road}, 2010)**

My father told me that when Grandfather came to Kansas, he lived in McCracken with the Neal family, where "Brownie" Neal worked him but also made him go to school. I have heard from more than one source that Grandfather made it as far as the third grade. He first worked odd jobs on farms and in the wheat fields, but Brownie required that he learn reading and writing. According to Dean John Birdsong (Herbert's nephew), Brownie's real name was Elmer Lee Neal, and he also was a railroader and Dean's great-uncle by marriage. According to my father, Grandfather first worked for the Missouri Pacific Railroad in McCracken, Kansas, as a "call boy," a role similar to that of a messenger or runner in a military unit. There were no telephones at this time. Grandfather's duty was to notify the engineers and crews of their schedule (a *run* or *trip)*. My father also told me that *"Dad [Herbert] worked as a night watchman in the section town of McCracken when he first came to Kansas."* (Birdsong H. M., 2010)

Discontent in the Heartland

In the early 1900s, there was a class or culture of men who rode the rails for various reasons. They were nicknamed the "IWWs"—or, as my father called them, the *"I Won't Work"* transients who frequented the rails. The term was attached to the Industrial Workers of the World (IWW), which was conceived and formed, in 1915 and had roots in Communist and Marxist ideology. Marxist doctrine was making its debut the world over during this time in history. The following passage gives the reader an idea of societal variance during these times.

Farmers in the years before the World War I faced thoroughly modern economic stresses and labor conflicts as the scale of their enterprises increased. By World War I, Midwestern and Great Plains farmers had come to rely on large pools of seasonal migrant labor, mostly unemployed urban workers from Chicago and other Midwestern cities, to harvest wheat or corn. Workers faced long hours and low wages, isolated in temporary camps without permanent homes or meeting places. The Industrial Workers of the World (IWW) union attempted to organize these "harvest stiffs." The radical "Wobblies" argued that wheat farmers were businessmen in a protected industry that, thanks to wartime government price supports, reaped large profits and returned none of that wealth to those who actually harvested their crop. (Kornbluh, 1968)

The methods to organize this ideology spread throughout the United States and into the wheat fields of Kansas and the wheat belt states by word and song. By today's standards, this movement would not be considered large, but it had a life of its own during these times. One typical venue of spreading the word was by song. Word and song of this organizing effort promulgated via the rail infrastructure throughout the area.

In 1915, the Industrial Workers of the World (IWW) established a branch union, the Agriculture Workers' Organization (AWO). The AWO organized temporary harvesters [were] known as "harvest stiffs" in railroad yards, migrant camps, and shelters. At its height in 1917, the AWO had more than 70,000 members, but like the IWW, it was undermined by President Woodrow Wilson's wartime attack on dissent and by local vigilante organizations. The AWO, like its parent organization, used folksongs, stories, and poetry to spread its message to migrants. One such song, "Harvest Land," by "TD and H," first appeared in the Little Red Songbook, a free booklet that IWW members regularly distributed to organizers and workers. Like most IWW songs, it set satirical lyrics to popular or traditional tunes, in this case, "Beulah Land." (Kornbluh, 1968). Even though this movement tried to become a major force in agriculture, it eventually became a lethargic influence in the central farmlands of America.

I heard my Grandmother Martha call the wandering men "hobos," and remember them coming to the back door asking for something to eat. It sticks in my mind that she once indicated that we were a "marked family" by word of mouth—that the Herbert Birdsong family of Hoisington was deemed generous and would feed a needy mouth during the hard times. I remember that these hobos sporadically would come to the back door and knock. This occurred even in the 1950s when I was a child. I was mesmerized by these strange men who came out of nowhere to knock on our back door to respectfully ask for something to eat. I continue to wonder what made these men wander and not settle.

In reading on this subject, I came across these fitting words of a Dr. Ben L. Reitman, who states, *"The hobo works and wanders, the tramp dreams and wanders, and the bum drinks and wanders."*

I surmise that the trains were the primary method of transportation of these men as they roamed the United States looking for work or whatever they were seeking. I am sure they gained intimate knowledge of the network of rails in America.

It seems that the I. W. W. at the time was a somewhat potent movement of the Socialist and Marxist ideology in the early nineteenth century as told in the American Heritage Magazine - Vol. 18, Issue 4, *"Here come the Wobblies."*

A tough problem for the I.W.W. was how to achieve "direct action" in the migrant workers' spread-eagle world. A factory or a mine could be struck. But how could the I.W.W.'s farmhands' union, the Agricultural Workers' Organizations, "strike" a thousand square miles of wheat field divided among hundreds of farmer employers?

The answer was, as the Wobblies put it, "To bring the strike to the job," or, more bluntly, sabotage. To the average American, sabotage conjured up nightmares of violence to property: barns blazing in the night, crowbars twisting the steel and wire guts out of a machine... But the I.W.W. leaders insisted that they had something less destructive in mind—merely the slowdown, the "conscientious withdrawal or efficiency," or, in working-stiff terms, "poor pay, poor work."

Still the I.W.W. leaders in the field pushed ahead with their tactics. The Agricultural Workers, to strengthen the threat of mass quitting by harvest hands, organized a "thousand-mile picket line" of tough Wobblies who worked their way through freight trains in the farm belt, signing up new members and unceremoniously dumping off any "scissorbills" or "wicks" who refused a red card. (Dr. Bernard A. Weisberger, 1967)

This historical backdrop gives us a temperature of the times in understanding the issues and concerns of the average American in the wheat belt and establishes a look at some of the issues that confronted my grandparents as they assimilated their lives into this region of America.

As technology increased and the use of cars and trucks on blacktop became prevalent, these wandering men used the railroad network less and less. The displacement of the steam engine by diesel technology in the 1950s seriously contributed to the decline of the wandering hobo. Steam engines had to make regular water stops, which allowed hoboes ready portals from which to access the intricate network of the railroads in the heartland. Many hobo camps were close to these water-tank stops. This was the case in McCracken, Kansas, where my grandfather and his brother began their careers. It was a section town and had a coal chute and a water tank for replenishing a steady stream of steam locomotives. (Birdsong D. J., Disscussion of Family, 2010) The advent of the diesel engine technology eliminated the need for frequent stops. Thus began the declining numbers of wandering men on the rails.

I have read that hobos' were tolerated in the 1930s and 1940s. In fact, some railroads would have one or two empty box cars to allow hobos access so they wouldn't break into sealed cars laden with marketable goods. This would seem to be a good strategy, considering the number of men that rode the rails in those early years.

I provide these short glimpses of history to display some of the issues of my grandparents' times and culture.

Establishing Residence

It was an established fact that Grandfather Herbert was a feisty little character who was not afraid of any man and would not back down from a confrontation. My father tells of the time when he had to take his turn in what we now term home *hospice* to care for his grandfather, Adam Giesick, in Otis, Kansas, since Adam was very sickly and expected to pass. When my father was taking his turn caring for his Grandfather Adam (the junior) in 1946, the past Methodist preacher of the Otis congregation, who was a good friend of his great-grandfather Adam, came to pay his respects. The preacher told my father that he had seen his father, Herbert, in action working on the railroad when Herbert confronted a rather large and burly IWW in the rail yard. The IWW hobo had indicated to him, "I will tell you what you are going to do..." Grandfather Herbert stepped up to the man, moved close to his face, pointed his finger in the man's chest, placed his other hand on his pocket pistol, and told him to get on the train and leave immediately. According to the preacher, the IWW man left immediately because he saw that Grandfather Herbert was *all business* and would not be intimidated. The pastor added, "He was a brave man to have confronted such a large man in front of all those other men." (Birdsong H. M., 2010)

Brothers James Christian Jr. and Herbert Monroe Birdsong, circa 1915-1917 (Birdsong D. J., 1915-1917)

I have heard several renditions from various family members of the story of how Grandfather Hiram came to settle in Kansas. The fact that his older brother Jim (James Christian Jr.) had already made the journey to Kansas and found work in the wheat fields was undoubtedly the deciding factor for him to leave Georgia and travel to

Kansas. It is known that not only were they close in age, but they also were close in their sibling relationship. Grandfather Hiram looked up to Jim for guidance and companionship. My father has said that his dad told him, "You could make a good living working in the wheat fields of Kansas." My father always maintained that Grandfather Hiram did not talk about his childhood; he sensed that he looked back on this as a very hard time. Hiram told my father that he and Jim were, "Shifted around with brother and sister, and worked very hard after his mother Mary Lou had died." Herbert told his son that he lived in a barn, which served as his bedroom. He also said that they worked from daylight to dusk doing the everyday things that people did back then. He related the time he got sunburned so badly that they put horse liniment on him to assuage the pain. From these snippets of family story, I assume that Jim and Herbert left Georgia in search of a better life than they experienced as young, orphaned boys. (Birdsong H. M., 2010)

I found an off-cycle census in the State of Kansas called "the decennial state census," which was required by law and was taken in on March 1, 1915. This census was the responsibility of the State Board of Agriculture and dealt with miscellaneous data such as agriculture, creameries, schools, libraries, and churches. It did not include run-of-the-mill data found on the standard census of every decade. This census enumerates Herbert Birdsong as boarding with the Neal family, Tom and Sarah Neal (56 and 55 years of age, respectively) in McCracken, Kansas. To supplement her husband's income, Sarah Neal ran a boarding home mainly for the railroad and harvest hands who frequented the town. Brother James (Jim) married into this family, marrying Opal Neal, the couple's granddaughter. Jim entrusted Grandfather Hiram to Elmer Lee "Brownie" Neal at first, Brownie was the son of Tom Neal, who was Missouri Pacific section chief in McCracken at the time. The census shows Grandfather's occupation to be an auto driver at the time (March 1, 1915), this probably syncs with him being the call boy mentioned earlier. My father speculates that "auto driver" meant he drove a drayage vehicle, delivering freight items to merchants and customers. The vehicle could have been a horse-drawn wagon or a motorized vehicle. It lists Grandfather Herbert's age as 19 years and notes that he was single, had been born in Georgia, came from Alabama as the last state (the column heading is, "Where from to Kansas naming state or territory of U.S."), and that his profession was an auto driver. (Government U. S., Kansas Decennial Census, 1915)

The earlier 1910 Census of Talbot County, Georgia, M. D. 876 Red Bone Township lists Herbert Birdsong as a "boarder," living with Will and Clyde Boggs on Talbotton Road, which is near Pleasant Hill, Georgia. Will was 31 years old and Clyde, his wife, was 23 years of age. Herbert was 15 years old and was listed as a "farm laborer" and "working hand." (Government U. S., Thirteenth Census, 1910)

This also gives another view of the approximate timeline when Grandfather arrived on Brother Jim's doorstep. Recall that it states in the 1915 decennial census that he had come from the state of Alabama. Speculation could be that Hiram spent some time with his older brother, Charley, in Alabama. Census taking was verbal, and he may have told the enumerator that the last place he was before coming to Kansas was Alabama. He could have been visiting Charley, who lived there. We do know that Charley ended up working and living in the Birmingham area of Alabama for the rest of his life. Also during this period was when Hiram claimed that his living quarter was a barn. The 1910 Census showed him living (boarding) and working at the Boggs's place in M. D. 876 Red Bone Township, Talbot County.

World War I Draft Registration

Herbert's draft registration card places him in Hoisington, Kansas, and was signed by him on May 31, 1917. He is shown as a locomotive fireman on the Missouri Pacific Railroad and of single status, medium build, and stout; with blue eyes, light colored hair, not bald, and not missing any limbs, legs, toes, digits, or being disabled.

In May 1918, Congress passed the Selective Service Act, which authorized the President to augment the draft of men into military service due to the situation in Europe at the time. The Selective Service System (SSS) came under the office of the Provost Marshal General and supervised the process of selection and induction during this period. The overall process was organized by state offices and then district boards, local boards (usually encompassing a county), and medical advisory boards to support the district and local boards.

WWI Draft Registration Card signed by H.M. Birdsong on May 31, 1917

These entities were charged with registering men, classifying them, and setting up the guidelines for manpower in certain industries and agriculture, as well as determining special family considerations of registrants, handling any appeals, setting medical fitness standards, determining the logical order of when each registrant would be called, and transporting the men to the training centers. There were three nationwide registrations carried out from 1917 through the end of 1918. From the date on Grandfather's card, it was obvious he registered on the first draft.

There were five WWI draft classifications. Potential draftees were Class 1 until they were evaluated for military service or their draft status was reclassified and established into a holding category and given a deferment for a specific situation or condition. After Class 1 was exhausted, men who were deferred in the remaining classifications (Class 2 through 4) would be called in the order of their availability and in the reverse order of need in social and economic life in this country. Class 5 was not subject to induction.

Each draft board used a set of standard "principles" to place men in the deferred classes, including dependency, sundry specific vocations, necessary agricultural and industrial workers, or moral disqualification. Alien citizens, termed alienage by the SSS, were placed in class 5...Necessary agricultural and industrial workers were classified in all classes "according to the degree of their skill and the relative necessity and importance of such an individual to a particular enterprise. In class 2 was placed a registrant found by his district board to be a necessary skilled farm laborer in a necessary agricultural enterprise or a necessary skilled industrial laborer in a necessary industrial enterprise. (Nudd)

As I researched this subject, my focus took me to the National Archives, where I found Grandfather Herbert's draft classification of Class II and a plausible explanation from the *Selective Service Regulations* (Act of Congress approved May 18, 1917) as to why he was placed in this category. Unlike with the Vietnam War, the draft classifications in WWI apparently were not as inclusive and easy to dodge. In fact, I gathered from my reading that our government was quite serious about drafting young men during those times. It was not easy to maneuver out of serving the nation during this war. There had to be a good reason for receiving a deferment.

In the manual under "Classification In Respect of Engagement in Industry and Agriculture," the following is transcribed:

C. Classification in Respect of Engagement in Industry and Agriculture.

To the District Boards will be entrusted the solution of one of the most vital problems of the war. Two things are to be accomplished--to raise armies, to maintain industries and agriculture. As the war proceeds more and more men will be required for the battle line, and yet there are certain industries that must be maintained to the end. Any considerable diminution of man power must interfere to some extent with industry...A balance must be struck and maintained between the military and the industrial needs of the Nation...it is the interest of the Nation solely that must be subserved; that the interest of individuals or associations of individual interest happens to coincide with the interest of the Nation, and furthermore, that the success of the Nation's military operations is the dominant object, to which the conservation of certain industries is related as one means to that end.

By placing the supply of skilled labor appurtenant to necessary industry and agriculture in Class II we leave (for the present, at least) available and unimpaired the entire body of men who have fitted themselves for effective engagement in necessary industry and agriculture and place in Class I only persons who are not so necessary for home activities as they are for the battle lines. To carry this principle into the field of unskilled labor and to place in

Class II unskilled labor engaged in necessary industries and agriculture would practically result in such serious inroads into the labor supply appurtenant to purely commercial, auxiliary, and other useful enterprises as to upset the economic balance of the Nation. For this reason unskilled labor cannot be segregated into a deferred class.

In pursuing this research, I received the list of men from Barton County on the WWI classification list from the National Archive. On the page that Grandfather Herbert was listed with 21 other men, he and only 3 others were classified as Classification II; the rest were Classification I. What did this mean at the time? I am only making an assumption from the documentation available. In viewing this particular list, it was clear that the number drafted exceeded those of Classification II in this particular instance. These facts coupled with the SS Regulations and with the logic (a test of reasonableness), that his job as a locomotive fireman placed him in the Classification II status due to the nation's industrial needs for this region, which meant he would be called later if there had been a need for more manpower on the battle lines. However, it is likely he was classified as essential to the nation's industrial (railroad) needs in the beginning of the war. Moreover, because the government had essentially nationalized the railroads, it is conceivable that a Classification II was assigned to most of the railroad employees. In addition, we all know the results of "the war to end all wars." (Government U. S., 1917)

After the armistice on November 11, 1918, (Grandfather's Hiram's twenty-third birthday), the activities of the SSS were shut down. On November 27, 1918, the

Provost Marshal General ordered that all organizations encompassed in the draft registration process be curtailed and the records sent to Washington, DC. All this processed paperwork now lies in our National Archive in Atlanta, Georgia.

The Masonic Lodge

This is an appropriate time in this family history to bring up the nickname of Grandfather Herbert. He was, as far as I know, called "Hiram" for most of his life, even though his given name was Herbert Monroe. His son (my father), whose given name is Hiram Monroe, told me that my grandfather was nicknamed Hiram by his fellow Masons, in honor of a historical Mason in the Masonic Lodge organization. Without getting into depth of Masonic ritual or history, Hiram Abiff, historically, was the Grand Master architect at the erection of Solomon's temple in early biblical times. He was the Master General Contractor by today's terms, who laid out daily work schedules and plans for the completion of the temple and had its design, configuring the total concept within his mind. Masonic ritual, dogma, and principal are much centered on this historical figure. According to my father, all the Masons at Hoisington Lodge No. 331, A. F. & A. M. felt an affinity for him and called him by the affectionate nickname of Hiram. Grandfather Hiram was a 32 degree Mason, as is shown in his Masonic certificate below. He achieved this level in the Masonic Lodge at an early age in 1920 and remained a trusted and loyal Brother of Hoisington Lodge No. 331 the rest of his life. I also have heard from various sources, including my mother, that, "He really did like the nickname Hiram!" (Giesick, 1974)

According to Dean J. Birdsong (Herbert's nephew), Herbert was also called "Hub," which was the short Southern pronunciation of Herbert. It was learned from Dean's father James that all Herbert's brothers and sisters referred to him as "Hub" this and "Hub" that! (Birdsong D. J., Disscussion of Family, 2010)

(Birdsong W. J., Certificate of 32 Degree Masonry - Herbert M. Birdsong, 1920)

In Masonic ritual, Hiram Abiff is not a worker of brass as in Scripture, but rather the Grand Master at the building of Solomon's temple. Each day, he lays out the work for the workmen to complete. There are Fellow crafts who work on the temple who are to be given the secrets of a Master Mason as compensation—when the temple is completed. (http://www.ephesians5-11.org/hiram.htm, 2010)

This Bible pictured below is my father's Bible presented to him by the Masonic Lodge after Grandfather Herbert passed. He has kept this Bible throughout his life:

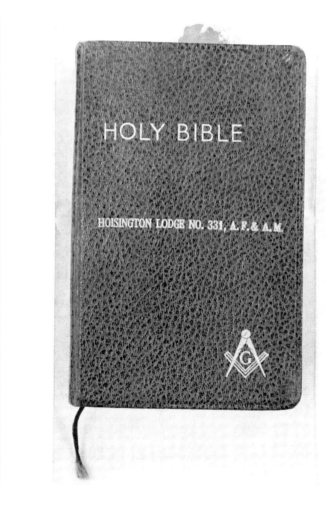

**Holy Bible presented by Hoisington Lodge No. 331
in 1950**

Holy Bible Preface (Front Matter) presented by Lodge No. 331

Grandfather was a devout Mason, dearly loved the organization, and was well thought of in the inner circle of Masonic brothers. My mother, W. Jean Birdsong, said of him, "He was a kind man and always took food to other needy families and would loan money to others when they needed it. He was always looking out for others not so fortunate." (Giesick, 1974)

In an excerpt from the preface of my father Hiram's Masonic Bible is the following passage, which I thought was befitting of my grandfather's legacy: *As faith in God is the cornerstone of Freemasonry, so, naturally, the Book which tells us the highest truth about God is its altar-light. The Temple of King Solomon, about which the history, legends, and symbolism of the Craft are woven, was the tallest temple of the ancient world, not in the grandeur of its architecture, but in the greatness of the truth for which it stood. In the midst of ignorant idolatries and debasing superstitions, the Temple on Mount Moriah stood for the Unity, Righteousness, and Spirituality of God. Upon no other foundation can men build with any sense of security when the winds blow and the floods descend.*

Therein our Fraternity is wise, building its Temple square with the order of the world and the needs and hopes of men, erecting its philosophy upon faith in spiritual verity and ruling its conduct by the immutable principles of moral law. While we may not say that Masonry is a religion, in the sense that it is one religion among many, it is none the less religious in its spirit and purpose: not simply a code of ethics, but a fraternity founded upon religious faith. (Joseph Fort Newton, The Bible and Masonry (Preface in THE HOLY BIBLE))

Additionally, Section IV of the preface of his Bible captures the essence of what I knew of my grandfather and what I learned about him through stories and family discussions that provided accounts of his character, demeanor, and strength.

It behooves every Mason, of every rite and rank, not only to honor the Bible as the Great Light of the Craft, but to read it, study it, live with it, love it, lay its truth to heart and learn what it means to be a man. There is something in the old Book--a sense of God, a vision of a moral order, a passion for purity, an austere veracity, a haunting pathos and pity--which, if it gets into a man, makes him both gentle and strong, faithful and free, obedient and tolerant, adding to his knowledge virtue, patience, temperance, self-control, brotherly love, and pity. The Bible is as high as the sky and as deep as the grave; its two great characters are God and the Soul, and the story of their life together is its everlasting romance. It is the most human of books, telling us the half-forgotten secrets of our own hearts, our sins, our sorrows, our doubt, and our hopes. It is the most Divine of books, telling us that God has made us for Himself, and that our hearts will be restless, unhappy, and alone, until we find our rest in Him whose will is our peace. (Joseph Fort Newton, The Holy Bible - Authorized King James Version, Copyright 1925)

Superstitious by Birth

Superstitions by definition are supernatural beliefs and/or notions that are entertained regardless of reason or knowledge. These practices are accepted by some people and discounted by others. Grandfather was one of those people who had deep beliefs in certain superstitions, for instance, Friday the 13th and, of course, black cats crossing his path. These preoccupations with the supernatural gained eminence in his mind most likely from his Southern roots.

Southerners are known for their rituals to avoid imagined evil or the untimely bad luck of such occurrences. Friday the 13th is regarded as a bad-luck day. According to my research, the superstition may have originated from Christian traditions and could be associated with the crucifixion of Jesus (which took place on a Friday), or the Last Supper that was attended by Judas, the thirteenth guest (Judas betrayed Jesus to his Roman enemies for 30 pieces of silver). In the beginning, Eve purportedly offered Adam the apple in the Garden of Eden on a Friday. Literature from the 17th century advised following the old saying, "Never set out on a journey on a Friday."

We can view superstitions in a number of ways. The more logical focus highlights this phenomenon as an empty belief system or blind faith with no logical basis for establishing it as reality. Alternatively, these beliefs can be viewed as being in the realm of the metaphysical. We can also view them as a watered-down version of a greater truth not yet known to us. Another perspective is to view superstitions with a foundational perception as linked with traditions of religious systems and passed through generations to the present.

Lighting three cigarettes on one C-ration match was a no-no in Vietnam. The author carried a Zippo lighter in Vietnam and can verify that it was bad luck to light more than one cigarette without first shutting the lid and then re-opening it to light another's cigarette. I am sure this type of simple superstition existed in the daily routines of most soldiers during both the Revolutionary War and Civil War. In addition, in Vietnam it was bad luck to speak about who might next be wounded or killed. The subject was taboo.

A combination of pagan and past Christian events, beliefs, and rituals has most likely shaped these paranormal traditions of superstitions. These beliefs have evolved throughout various societies and taken on an importance of foreknowledge. This, as I understand from my family, allowed my grandfather to take timely action to avert bad happenings. For example, I understand that after a train wreck he was involved in during the mid-1930s, his belief in superstitions was actualized to an even greater degree. According to my father, the train wreck happened on a Friday, and it was on the 13th day of that month. After reviewing all the wreckage and events, Grandfather related that the 13th car went off the track that caused the wreck. This, according to my father, made such an impression on Hiram that from that time on, he would not schedule a train trip or run to Horace on a Friday the 13th. Of course, Friday the 13th typically occurs only once or twice a year on the Gregorian calendar, but some years have as many as three Fridays on the 13th. I am sure my grandfather was serious in wanting to avert any unwelcome event that might occur because of this belief system.

Later in this book, I will describe as completely as possible my grandfather's professional life on the Missouri Pacific Railroad, and his and my grandmother's assimilation into the family-building years. It now is time to turn the focus to my Grandmother Martha and her family origins.

Herbert Monroe "Hiram" Birdsong, 1920s (Birdsong W. J., Photo of Herbert M. Birdsong, 1920s)

PART II: OUR GIESICK FAMILY

Chapter 4 ~ Giesick Family Origins

"The past is a Foreign Country: They do things differently there." *These* words, written by L. P. Hartley at the beginning of his book, *The Go-Between;* seem a fitting and poignant theme for introducing the osmotic passage of my grandmother's people from the old country to America. The first known recorded data of the Giesicks began in Brunnental, Russia. Today it is known as Krivojar, Russia, and is a small agricultural community in the farm regions of the Volga River inside Russia. The closest major city is Volgograd. Brunnental is situated to the east of the Volga River. It is a river-bottom valley with plenty of water, which led to its name–*well-valley.* Brunnental is in what is known as the Samara region and is called the Wiesenseite (valley or meadow-side). Its rolling hills are known as *steppeland,* which stretches all the way to the Ural Mountains and south to Tsaritsyn (Volgograd). The west side of the river is referred to as Bergseite (hilly side), and its hills merge with the many level areas. This entire river-bottom area is well suited for grain farming. The approximate latitude is 50° 51' N and the longitude: 46° 29' E.

History of the Volga

How did this region originate and grow? In 1763 the Russian Empress, Catherine II (often called *Catherine the Great)* invited foreigners except Jews of neighboring countries to bring their skills and settle in Russia. The newcomers were encouraged to develop the remote region of the rich river-bottom land of the Volga River. This manifesto was a great success, and large populations of starving farmers, skilled tradesmen, and veteran soldiers from surrounding countries signed up for emigration to the area. Although agents traveled throughout Europe recruiting émigrés, the largest numbers came from the German-speaking regions. These areas had just witnessed the Seven Years War, and its citizens were ripe for any semblance of economic opportunity, independence, and security that was available. From 1764 through 1767, approximately 25,000 to 28,000 Germans left Germany to settle in Russia and the colonies. A much smaller population of French, Dutch, Italian, Polish, and Swedish also homesteaded these new lands and began farming beside the German majority. (Webmaster, 2010)

From what areas of Germany did the German farmers, tradesmen, and soldiers come? I found that recruited emigrants converged at assembly points in cities such as Regensburg, Freiburg, and Rosslau, to name a few. Under the guidance of commissioners, they often traveled to Luebeck, a city on the Baltic Sea, and sometimes to Danzig where they set sail for Russia. Marriages, births, baptisms, and deaths took place in these ports of departure. Sometimes, challenges such as frozen rivers, insufficient funds, and crowded ships prolonged their leaving. Germans came from the regions of Wetterau, Vogelsberg, Spessart, Rhoen, Odenwald, Hessen, among others. In addition, certain areas such as Hessen, some villages' populations totally disappeared and reappeared in the Volga River Colonies. (Miller, 2010)

This simple map, which I annotated, shows the German-Russian settlement area of the village of Brunnental, Saratov region, within Russia, which was colonized by the Germanic people. The area west of the Volga River was known as Berseite (mountain side), and east of the river was Wiesenseite (meadow side). The map is from *CIA World Fact* book (public domain).

Life in the Volga Colonies

What was life in the Brunnental region like? Following are excerpts from a history of Brunnental written by Jakob Mohrland in 1986. Jakob left the area and went to Germany in the early 1940s due to events that are not entirely clear. The manuscript he wrote has been translated into English from German, and his passages are in the context of the Germanic tongue. The intent in using his history is to give the reader an idea of the geography, economy, and culture of the Volga River colonies. In addition, it will highlight what my grandmother's people experienced during these times. (Mohrland, 1986)

The colonists, who founded the first colonies on both sides of the Volga River, are in the walks of life from 85 to 90 years, when even with many setbacks, became prosperous. The colonies became always more beautiful and well off. For that reason, the colonists' families always had many children. Because of that, there prevailed already in 1840, a large demand for land for the grownup sons who wanted to become independent farmers. (Mohrland, 1986)

At the end of this chapter is the Ancestry Chart of the Giesick family, which reinforces the proclivity toward large families during these times. Likewise, the emigrants to this river-bottom area focused on developing an agriculture that would become the breadbasket of the area. This land was suitable for growing many of the grains that accompanied the Volga-German immigrants to the United States to be cultivated in Kansas, Nebraska, Oklahoma, South Dakota, and North Dakota. Here began the cultivation of a "brain trust," a developing of the first of many techniques, methodologies, and expertise in farming large crops, especially wheat.

Brunnental was founded in 1855 (according to the statement of the Homeland Almanac of 1955). It lies almost exactly in the middle between Seelmann and Krasny-Kut. From Seelmann to Brunnental it is 35 kilometers. I am of the opinion that those colonists who founded their village sought a favorable site… the scouts, who sought suitable arable land for the new village location, found a place with a light flat valley where three river-like canals came together into a larger canal. The larger canal, in the springtime, on account of the snow melt and heavy rain flow, the scouts saw in advance that this area would be favorable…For the new founded colonies, these canals were of great significance because they could be used for the collection and preservation of water…I learned this from the older people who said that the new colonists of Brunnental constructed dams on the canals right away. (Mohrland, 1986)

The climate of the Volga Valley was one of extremes, similar to that of the U.S.–Canada border in the region of North Dakota, Montana, or perhaps Wisconsin, which is on that same latitude as the Volga Valley. Nevertheless, the soil was fertile and conducive for raising grain crops. The winters were brutal, and keeping warm was a high priority.

To keep from freezing in the cold weather in winter, farmers wore fur coats made of sheepskin with high collars, when they made trips to Seelmann with horse and sleds. The fur coat tailors came every winter from the surrounding

Russian villages in order to sew for the German farmers. These fur-coat tailors were big specialists in their profession. They have lived among the farmers a long time and were given good board and room. The sewing was paid for. They came mostly in groups of 2 to 3 men and went by orders, from house to house... (Mohrland, 1986)

This region was dependent on its snowmelt, rainfall, and water channels. Its agriculture (economic system) was the focus of everyone in the region. Everything centered on crops and a barter system.

Wheat, rye, oats, and barley were mainly raised in Brunnental, while smaller portions of sunflowers, watermelons and melons were also raised. Very few potatoes were raised because the climate was too dry for potatoes. One could only raise potatoes in moist deep earth and for those the farmer raised only enough for himself...Some fruit was raised...but without importance. The people of Brunnental received fruit from the hilly-side farmers, every summer. Every summer from the middle to the end of June, the hilly-side farmers would come first with wagon loads of cherries and later apples...The Brunnental farmers' didn't buy the fruit. It was exchanged for wheat or rye – measure for measure. The hilly-side farmers drove the length of the street and called out, 'Fruit exchange, tit for tat, small for large'. It was meant like this: For one sack of apples, one sack of wheat; or 1 pail of apples, 1 pail of wheat. The business went well and for both there was satisfaction. (Mohrland, 1986)

Vegetables were the responsibility of the individual farmer. Tomatoes, cucumbers, carrots, beets, beans, peas, and other foods were cultivated in the gardens of the farmers. Many of the vegetables and fruits (such as watermelons and applies) were pickled for the wintertime. Sauerkraut also was a mainstay food supplement in the wintertime. (Mohrland, 1986)

Religion played an important role in this community and was the cornerstone and foundation of the farm society. Religion in the eighteenth century went through major discord and reformation, and as a result, the colonists organized their villages and towns around their preferred religion. The primary worship centers of the area fell into three religious groups: Lutheran, Roman Catholic, and the Reformed Church (Christian, Protestant denomination). Brunnental was essentially of the Lutheran persuasion. Later we find that some of the family immigrants to Rush County, Kansas, broke away from the Lutheran church and began their allegiance to the Methodist religion. This schism would cause discord for many years to come.

Donald Hergert, my grandmother's nephew who now lives in the Duluth, Minnesota area, sent Grandmother Martha a letter and photocopy of the history of a popular hymnal he owns that is dated 1844. The hymnal came from Brunnental and was given to him by Samuel Giesick's wife Ella (Hergert). It accompanied the family all the way from Russia. The article he included in his letter reads as follows:

The circumstances and conditions peculiar to the Volga colonial area that led to the consociation of the two faiths must include the creation of a common hymnal in 1816 for use in all evangelical colonies. It replaced an assortment of 20 or so publications brought by the settlers from various regions of the Germanies. The new book contained an exceptionally well-balanced collection of 823 hymns in the first edition, all printed without notes. By 1834, when the third series came off the press at Dorpat (Yuryev), located about 160 miles southwest of St. Petersburg, the number of lyrics had grown to 878. The twenty-first edition, appearing in 1905, still was printed in Dorpat, still with 878 hymns, and still without notes...

The popular hymnal carried an imposing title: "Collection of Christian Songs for Public and Household Devotions for Use in the German Evangelical Colonies on the Volga." It will be noted that this explicatory appellation did not associate the hymnal with any single Protestant group. It was used in the Brotherhood prayer meetings as well as in Lutheran and Reformed churches. The third edition stressed the ecumenical aspect by carrying this line: 'Assembled by the Pastors of the Evangelical Colonies on the Volga'...

Together with the Bible and one of the two catechisms, this Wolga Gesangbuch formed the omnipresent bibliographical trinity in almost every Protestant colonist's home, and for many years the three constituted the only reading material to be found in most of them. The hymnal was carried proudly tucked under the arm of a man strolling to church or prayer meeting; the women carried it with sprig of fragrant leaves or a small corsage projecting from under its cover... (Even the occasional colonist who was unable to read proudly carried the Gesangbuch to church!)
(Hergert, Letter to Aunt Martha, 1988)

Donald further states …Do *you remember seeing it as a child? There is a lot of scribbling in it – mother (Grandmother Martha's sister, Mary) wrote her name in it – evidently, when she was a child. I suspect it was brought over by Grandpa Giesick . His name appears in it several times in German script – Adam Giessick – the strange thing is that <u>Giessick</u> is spelled with 2 s'. There are many other things written that are barely discernable, including the village of Brunnental and the year (Jahr) 1880. It's interesting to speculate about.* (Hergert, Letter to Aunt Martha, 1988)

Thoughts of Immigrating

Why and how did the Giesicks immigrate to America? I will speculate, review, and research other histories to help visualize these times and journeys. Grandmothers' nephew, Donald Hergert has contributed heavily to the gathering of the Giesick family history and lore. I regret that I did not interview my grandmother or her brothers about their early lives when I was younger. It is something that one typically does not think about in their youth. However, drawing from some of the recorded family writings and histories of other immigrants, I hope to illustrate as well as expose the colonists' and our ancestors' general mindset. One of the few areas that are heavily settled by Germans from the Volga colonies is Rush County, Kansas. I found this interesting commentary on the Center for Volga German Studies website, which lists the names of the families that came here from Russia. Notice our listed surname, *Giesick.*

History of Otis, Rush County, Kansas

Otis is the easternmost town of Rush County founded by Volga Germans. Before Otis became a town, there were Volga German settlements called Scheuerman (to the west) and Schöntal (to the north). Early Volga German immigrants to come to the Otis area included the Scheuerman, Brack, Wertz, Appel, Fuchs, Ochs, Miller, Krumm, Luft, Stang, Steitz, Hergert, Muth, Giesick, Hartman, Wirtz, Krause, Helin, Repp, Krunch, Ott, Schmidt, Moore, Rothe, Lebsack, Rudy, Kerb, Avis, Mootz, Rodie, and Sohm families.

Volga German Congregations
Lutheran
Methodist
Reformed (Webmaster C. , 2010)

The many varied personal reasons for immigrating to a new country such as the U.S. (in this case, the state of Kansas) is certainly noted in history. This selected writing vividly points out and explains the political climate in Russia at the time. It further highlights the desires and vision of not only a Mr. Athanasius Karlin, but also reveals the moral character and soul of the typical colonist's thinking. The date of this departure from Russia was on October 10, 1875. (Karlin, 2010)

The Wolga is one of the nicest rivers I saw. The river is 1 ½ Werft or a mile broad; in Spring it flooded the coast even to our place where we lived and the water tore much of the embankment away that we were forced one day to move our farm buildings further back. Katharinenstadt was situated on the meadow-site and had much nice land as pastures for the village flocks, for horses Dabon, cows and sheep Dabonen. ...Katharinenstadt was a nice village but by now it had grown to be a city. It had nice stores, a big market place. Every Monday was market-day and all kind of goods was sold. There was a very big lumberyard near the Wolga river, and 40 or more granaries (wheat Amagaren). The wheat was shipped by boats along the Wolga to the cities. Katharinenstadt had 3 big beautiful stone-churches. The Lutheran, a Russian church was the biggest and nicest. Our Catholic church came next; the pastor was Father Raymund Andreasjekowitsch, a Polish priest. He left the parish the same fall we moved away, after having attended to the community for 25 years...

The reasons for our emigration were first, not enough land and second, the successive emperors did not keep the promise which Empress Katharine had once made to the Germans. (Karlin, 2010)

Mr. Karlin writes that the Volga Germans were to start reporting to the Russian military service in 1874. His brother would be inducted by fall of 1875, so they decided to emigrate at once. He also points out that they were afraid of losing their freedom of religion. The priests were ordered to write down the words of every sermon to be inspected by Russian officials. These were the main reasons they decided to leave their present situation.

Two representatives from this community were sent to America, and they ended up traveling to Larned, Kansas. When they reported to the colonists, the area was presented

105

as "wild and strange," but they all decided nevertheless to start selling out and making plans to migrate immediately.

We all went to Mass and Holy Communion... Somebody came into the church, I guess it was Andreas Mayer, and said we must hurry; the boat is ready for Saratow. When we came home we found our farmyard crowded as if it would go to a funeral...many tears were shed and many a kiss given. I still remember the farewell song which we often used to sing when someone went traveling:

Prepare, Brothers, and be strong
Departure day is here
Our hearts beat heavily in our breasts
We journey over land and sea
To America, the free.
At Russia's border we stretch our hand
To you, beloved fatherland
And with a kiss express our thanks
For all the care and food and drink
Which you provided us.
And the mighty sea waves break
Upon our ship
We will still sail on at peace
For God is here, as God is there
And he is always with us. (Karlin, 2010)

It is not a well-known historical fact that these German colonists prospered in the early to mid-1800s in the Volga colonies. They grew in numbers and prospered very well through hard work and determination as they enjoyed their newfound state of being in a strange and inhospitable land.

Because the colonists thrived and were increasing in number, they soon were regarded with alarm. On June 4, 1871, Tsar Alexander II issued a decree by taking away most rights and privileges they were afforded in Catherine II's manifesto during the late 1700s. They were no longer called *colonists* but were referred to as *settlers*, which was an affront to their German pride.

Very little history was recorded or written during this time, leading up to this decree by Tsar Alexander II. Life had been fulfilled with family building, culture building, and colony building in the fertile river valley of the Volga. Men were exempt from military service, and few people ventured away from the area. Life was good, but laced with hard work. This changed during the 1870s.

A second decree on January 13, 1874, establishing a lottery for conscripting the young men into the tsar's military, was issued by the tsar. This news traveled like wildfire throughout the colonies, causing much alarm and uncertainty. Catherine's Second Manifesto had in it a provision for the colonists to quit being a colonist. The requirement was a tax to be paid on their property upon exiting Russia.

The Russian government finally issued a release clause, but a 10 percent tax on the property had to be finalized before passports were permitted.

The Volga Germans who had chosen to leave now collectively decided that before immigrating to another place, they would send representatives to carefully select new colonies.

These scouts that explored the central United States came back to Russia to report their findings, bringing with them soil samples, prairie grass, currency, and a variety of documentation and descriptive literature. Eventually, some stayed in the Volga colonies and some even ventured out to Siberia, where land was cheap and still available and the Codex was not enforced, since Russia was interested in developing this region. Nevertheless, a large number of these hearty Germans packed up their belongings and started the long trek to a faraway land that was just opening up to immigrants.

The Long Journey to America

I have heard various stories of the family's trip by ship to America, including that a child was lost and buried at sea, but I do not have verification of that obviously major and traumatic event. We can speculate as to the distress they must have felt. In a personal letter to my Grandmother Martha (Giesick) Birdsong, her nephew Donald Hergert documents (notates) in writing on an ancestry chart what she had told him earlier: "According to Aunt Martha (Giesick) Birdsong, the Conrad Giesicks (Martha's Uncle) had a young son who died and was buried at sea during the family immigration to the U.S.A. in mid-1886. His order in the family would probably have been #1 or 2." (Hergert, Letter to Aunt Martha, 1988)

Grandmother's father, Adam, had two brothers who came over from Russia. Their names were Conrad ("Coon"), and Wilhelm ("Bill"). Conrad was born in 1862; Adam

(Martha's father) was born on November 12, 1865, and Wilhelm was born in 1868. Adam and Bill are buried in Otis, Kansas, and Conrad is buried in Leoti, Kansas. They married as follows:

Conrad Giesick ~ Anna Catherina Windecker, 1880

Adam Giesick ~ Maria Kathrina Hergert, 1883

Wilhelm Giesick ~ Mary Elsessar, 1896

Ancestry Chart by Donald Hergert, nephew of Martha Giesick (Hergert, American Historical Society of Germans from Russia, 1987)

The trip to America from Russia was not an easy journey. Again, I am drawn to the stories and writings of Athanasius Karlin, whose history is available in the database of the Kansas State Historical Society. His people settled in

Catherine, Kansas, which is within 30 miles of Otis, Kansas, the homestead of the Giesick family. Catherine is located off Interstate 70 northeast of Hays, Kansas. Characteristic of the Volga Germans, the name of villages and towns were exact copies of their roots in Russia. *Karlin* comes from Katherinestadt in Russia, which translates to *Catherine* in English. I have chosen to use Karlin's written thoughts to parallel the probable thinking of our Giesick ancestors.

In his writing, his reminiscence is on the banks of the Volga River, where the main vessel they were to board was anchored in the middle of the river. It was referred to as a Contor type of boat. Their luggage and belongings were ferried by means of little boats (*laotgas*) to the Contor boat. The first part of the journey was by this boat to Saratow, where they were to board a train. (Karlin, 2010)

...Our travel company for America consisted of us and 8 persons, Michael Mayer, Justus Bissing together with [his] wife and their sons: Alois, Justus, Jakob, Alexander, and Peter. Futhermore, Friedrich Koerner with wife and sons: Friedrich, Paul, Phillip, Alois, Peter (John had been drafted), and daughters Emilie and Anna...

We disembarked at 3 P.M. and went to Ludwig Korner's restaurant, and there we met the emigrants from Herzog who also want to go to America...They wanted us to stay another day and go with them together by train. But we didn't...So we stayed only to the morning of October 11, got our tickets from Saratov over Tambow, Koslow, Srjasi, Orel, Smolensk, Witebsk to Wersbolow, the border-town of Russia. Here, the passports were examined and tickets bought for over the border to Eydkunen, the German border-town, a quarter mile from the Russian border…

…It was October 11, 1875 according to Russian time, according to American October 23, when we took final leave from our friends at the station of Saratow… We boarded the train and it headed west into the unknown future. We were having a nice ride without any stops till Orel. Here we got out for a rest, since Russian railway wagons are no American Pullman car or coach. They are small with narrow wooden benches, sometimes overcrowded and by no means pleasant. We did some shopping in Orel, bought some bread and some meat and other things. We got again in the train and on it went till we arrived in Berlin and that was on October 15, American calendar, Oct 27, because Russia is 12 days behind the time. We thought the Russians to be rough people who treated us roughly; it was nothing compared with the Germans in Berlin. They are surely the roughest we ever met. We stayed two days in Berlin in order to get the necessary information about the boat lines for our crossing…We were advised to go via Bremen to Baltimore. Our Russian money we got exchanged into American currency, getting for a Russian Rubel 70 cents…

Fritz Huseman, our innkeeper in Bremen had arranged for us, and the Catharinenstadter and Bergseiter boys who were with us, a room in the middle of the steamer. He said there will be not so much rocking. And he was right…

We were already 2 weeks on sea and the boat battling with storms and waves could not get ahead. One day it was on the 16th of October our boat made only three miles headway, no one was allowed on deck because the waves went over the boat; 17-18 days passed and no sign of land, the rations became smaller and smaller. The passengers protested and went to the Captain scolding on account of the little food and of having said to us we will land in two weeks and by now 18 days have gone by and no land yet. The Captain, a very understanding man said, 'Good people, you see yourself how the weather is, if I am too hard on the ship by going faster, something might break on the machines and none of us will reach the shore. I am responsible for your lives. And I like to live too. In the nicht of the 18th during the storm, my brother Jakob's wife gave birth to a baby. It was hard on the mother and she suffered some harm for the rest of her life; never been a well woman... At last, in the afternoon of November 22, we heard the calls, land; land; we see land. And in the morning of November 23, 1875 came the pilot and took over the steering of our boat leading her into the pier of Baltimore. (Karlin, 2010)

Most immigration into the United States during the 1800s and early 1900s was through the eastern portals of America. Imagine coming to a strange, free land and thinking of hope for your future and of settling your family while establishing your footprint on the landscape. How exciting this must have been, yet frightening. This mentality slowly forged this great nation during the twentieth century.

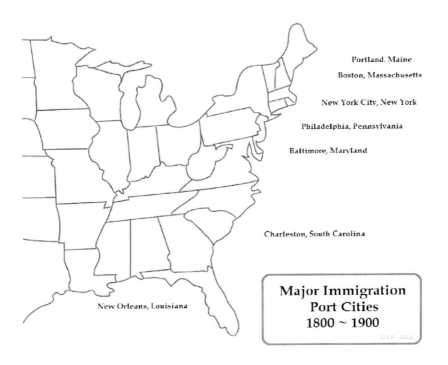

Portland, Maine

Boston, Massachusetts

New York City, New York

Philadelphia, Pennsylvania

Baltimore, Maryland

Charleston, South Carolina

Major Immigration
Port Cities
1800 ~ 1900

New Orleans, Louisiana

Ports of Entry ~ 1800s

Journey into the Heartland

When the Karlins arrived and went through Customs, they met up with the leader of the Herzoger emigrants, who had already arranged to go with land agent, C. B. Schmitt of the Atchinson, Topeka, and Santa Fe Railroad, on to Topeka, Kansas, and from there to look over the available land for sale. In route, they encountered the first of many hardships that were to come.

Because on our route (over St. Louis) at every stop, someone else of every family ran off the train in order to buy bread, but could never get enough. No baker anywhere had enough bread in store for 500 hungry people. Only the first ones who came to the bakery-shop would get some bread and the rest went away sadly without anything... (Karlin, 2010)

When they arrived in Topeka, they all lived together in an old vacated hotel. It was made of stone and was not big enough for 500 people.

The toilets got in these three days so filled up, that it was terrible to go in... (Karlin, 2010)

In the next few days, Karlin's family rented a two-story house for all of his people. The men of the family had to look for work and found some at the local farms, husking corn.

We did not make much, because we did not understand how to husk properly. 25 cents that was all we could earn a day. We got 3 cents for a husked bushel. We had to take from home our food for the day. The farm was 3 miles outside the city... (Karlin, 2010)

The Settlement

The new immigrants made a few trips out into the interior of Kansas with land agent C. B. Schmitt in search of land tracts. On the first trip they ventured out to Great Bend and Larned, finding the ground too expensive at five dollars per acre. That was not within the price range they were willing to pay, and there seemed to be not enough land for the number of people included in the colony. These trips were paid for by the Atchison, Topeka, and Santa Fe railroad land company. Returning to Topeka, they met with A. Roedelheimer, a land agent for the Union Pacific. A trip was arranged to Fort Hays, Kansas. The first land they looked at was between Hays and Ellis on Hogback, now Yocemento (Hogback or Yocementom, a small hill west of Hays). It was not suitable...*They found the place not big enough either for the erection of two villages like Herzog and Catharinenstadt should be some day, after all the other friends who still were in Russia, had come over...*

Discouraged, they returned to Hays... Mr. Roedelheimer said he has some more land northeast of Hays, perhaps we would like that. There will be enough Heimstadteland and we shall let you have the railroad site at two dollars the acre with 11 years term for payment and at seven % interest. Moreover, the railroad company will be willing to transport all your goods from Topeka or Kansas City and whatever you buy during one year, free of charge. And this the company did actually. And so they made the trip to North-fork, where there is now Catherinenstadt and Herzog... Hence we decided, when the majority of the other ones will agree with us, we shall settle there. (Karlin, 2010)

While this search for land was in progress, it became an unspoken fact that the new settlers would indeed stay in this new land. For most, it was now a matter of finding the right land at an affordable price. This seemed to be largely a group decision based on the consensus of the members of the new colony—that most of them could cluster within a close proximity. The decision to stay was imminent, and the process of establishing roots began once most of the Volga Germans had looked at the land.

During the three months we stayed in Topeka, it became known that we shall remain in Kansas and intended to buy horses and cows. From all sides of the country there were horses for sale. At first old and crippled ones, but as we didn't buy them, the Americans said, 'See the Russians, they understand something about horses,' and brought us better, even very good ones to the market. (Karlin, 2010)

This community began like other villages and settlements throughout the high plains of Kansas during the late 1800s. The forging of the community foundations had been time-tested, and now the work was beginning in building the breadbasket of the United States of America. In Kansas, a new day was dawning.

We bought the wagons and plows in Kansas City, a Studebaker Wagon, 75 Ds. [dollars], and two Brake-plows 18 Ds. apiece. A carload of timber had to be bought too, for three houses, ours, Bissings and Koerners. The price was 15 Ds. per 1000 for the coarse wood and Ds. 20 for floorings and ceilings.nce we got free transportations from the R.R. Co. for one year did we buy enough flour for two years, as we could not expect any harvest the first year. The price for flour should have been Ds. 2.50 a hundred lb, but got it for Ds. 1.25 and we bought 5000 lbs. Having done enough buying, we had to pack it and load the freight car and then, the train went on, bringing us nearer and nearer to our goal." (Karlin, 2010)

Threshing Machine at Giesick Farm, 1900s (Birdsong W. J., Wheat Harvest Giesick Farm, Early 1900s)

A Settlement is Born

As the supplies were gathered, the work began, establishing a new community of homesteaders:

Each house was planned 28 feet long and 18 feet wide, the inside walls 6 feet high and two half-windows into each wall and one front door...the roof got covered with boards and sod on the top. We worked together, i.e., us, the Bissing and Koerner boys, the old Gustel Vetter (cousin)... Down in the Creek we dug the community well and now there was Catharinenstadt created, the first accomplishment in North America, Ellis County, Kansas. We had lived in Hays in the old store for a month and seven days. (Karlin, 2010)

The first houses that Volga Germans built on the plains of Kansas were made of sod. Using the technology of the *brechpflug* (sod-busting plow), a long strip of prairie soil was cut and formatted into individual brick-like squares. The topsoil had never been dug up and its grass, roots, and tight soil formed a piece of hard sod that could be layered to provide a natural insulation and protection from the elements. The sod was placed on roofs and walls that were reinforced with the coarse lumber that was purchased by the colonists. These types of weather-tight shelters (called *Simolinkas* and/or *Semljankis*) had been used by the Volga Germans on the steppes of Russia, and were constructed quickly and cheaply. Inside, the *Simolinkas* was like other sod houses—dark and cool in summer, and dark and warm in winter. The inside walls were plastered with mud, reinforced with prairie grass, and sometimes whitewashed. (Karlin, 2010)

The Homestead – A New Beginning

I remember hearing my Grandmother Martha telling me of the dirt floors in these sod huts and of using animal blood on the floors to harden them, which made them easy to sweep. These facts are further reinforced in a letter from nephew Donald Hergert to Grandmother Martha on August 7, 1987:

Did you know that Grandpa Giesick and his brother Conrad lived a couple of years on farms 2 miles west of Albert, Kansas? This was around 1890 to 1892, just before they moved to the farms west of Otis.

Was grandpa & grandma's first house on the Otis farm a sod house? Mother remembered living in a sod house in which the floors had been hardened by mixing the dirt with animal blood to make it possible to sweep them.

I have a couple of pictures Irene gave to me. When I have access to a good copy machine, I will make copies to send to you. One is the picture of grandma, you & grandpa in front of the Otis farm house. It was taken during the summer of 1910. The other one is your confirmation class picture. Perhaps you could help me identify some of the individuals. I used to know quite a few but have forgotten most of them. (Hergert, Letter to Martha (Giesick) Birdsong, 1987)

New Arrivals

The Kansas prairie was Indian country in the mid-1800s, and some military posts were constructed to patrol the area. Fort Hays and Fort Larned (down-line from Fort Leavenworth which was located along the Missouri River) were the predominant posts in this immediate locale, which provided some security for a venturing soul who would meander into this new wilderness. They were there also to monitor traffic along the Santa Fe Trail. From 1821 until the 1880s, the Santa Fe Trail was a major overland route between Independence, Missouri, and Santa Fe, New Mexico. I distinctly remember the region as being referred to in our 1950s school history lessons as "the Great American Desert."

In his book, *Comrades,* Stephan E. Ambrose writes about brevetted General George Custer and his life after the Civil War when he took charge of the Seventh Calvary Regiment at Fort Hays, Kansas, in the 1870s. He writes, *"The 7th Cavalry was ordered into Kansas, Colorado, and neighboring states to fight Indians and prepare the way for the coming of the railroad... How tough this duty was in the dry, (almost) waterless, homeless desert can be best understood by considering the deserters--more than 10 percent of Custer's men took off rather than endure it."* (Ambrose, 2000)

To give you a flavor of the local history and the eventual settlement of this dry land farming area, I will turn to a book compiled by the Rush County Book Committee (Rush County Historical Society) in 1976 titled, *Rush County Kansas: A Century in Story and Pictures, The township of Pioneer in which Otis is located is the oldest township (1870) in the county... The first Post Office in the county was Economy in this same township. This was established in 1871. Economy was served by a stagecoach out of Great Bend... In 1875 Pioneer Township had a population of 210, the largest in the county, total population at that time being 451.* (Haning, 1976)

Pioneer Township is the area where Adam and Mary Giesick, father and mother of Martha Giesick, settled and eventually passed on their home to his son Samuel and wife Ella. The acreage they homesteaded and cultivated is four miles west and one mile north of Otis, Kansas, on State Highway 4. It is called "the Homestead" by my grandmother. Otis, Kansas, can be *geotagged* (a video camcorder plus global positioning system term) at the approximate latitude 38° 32' 6" N and longitude 99° 3' 8" W.

There was no railroad in the county as yet; the Kansas Division of the Union Pacific was passing to the north through Hays and the Atchison, Topeka, and Santa Fe was to the south passing through Larned. (This explains why our early settlers from Russia came up north from Larned. They had first stopped in Kansas at Topeka.).

By 1874, Kansas was a state of thirteen years. Increased population was being actively sought. Railroad promoters and land promoters were canvassing American and European sources in search of new settlers. It may be hard for the present day reader to realize the zeal and enthusiasm of railroad people vying for first place and greatest resources... It was between the years of 1875 and 1880 that population in Rush County increased rapidly. The two prime elements in the development of the area were not accidental. They were actively promoted. That is the coming of farm families hopeful of carving out a prosperous living from the soil and the rapid development of railroad transportation across the area were deliberately encouraged. (Haning, 1976)

The railroads during this period were given land by the government as incentive to expand their reach and coverage. To promote their services, the railroads did a lot of planning and advertising throughout the eastern seaboard and around Europe, shining a favorable light on these immense land holdings. These promoters of land and transportation brought not only economic progress to the area but also transplanted enormous numbers of habitants—industrious people coming from Russia and Europe to this frontier area who were looking for a new life in which they could prosper.

Word spread throughout the colonies of the Volga region in Russia, and scouts were sent to this mid-continent area to check it out. Not only did they come to mid-America, they also went to Canada and South America to look for available land and report back to their communities in Russia. It was only a matter of time before these hardworking Germans would immigrate to Kansas, Nebraska, Colorado, Oklahoma, and other areas of the United States. These regions were very similar to their homelands along the Volga River, and they would be able to resume their lives with newfound freedoms that were being slowly eroded in Russia. (Haning, 1976)

Confirmation Class Picture, Otis, Kansas
(Catechism Methodist Church)

In the partial photo above, (20 students graduated from this Confirmation class), a teenage Martha (Giesick) Birdsong is on the lower right. The photograph was photocopied by Donald Hergert and shared with the family. (Hergert, Confirmation Class Picture Otis, Kansas)

**Martha Giesick (on the left) as a young woman
(Birdsong W. J., Martha Giesick with unknown woman,
1917-1920)**

My grandmother attended a one-room schoolhouse located not far from their homestead farm in Pioneer Township, Rush County. My mother, W. Jean Birdsong, saved and passed on to me many documents that provide important clues to my grandparents' past. Following is a photo of a pamphlet from 1912 titled, "Souvenir" - 1912 - *"Of all the Memories of the past, School Memories are the ones that last."*

**Souvenir School Pamphlet from Pioneer Township,
Rush County, Kansas (Cover)**

Listed in the document are the names of the students of
School District No. 48. This was a one-room schoolhouse
on the prairie.

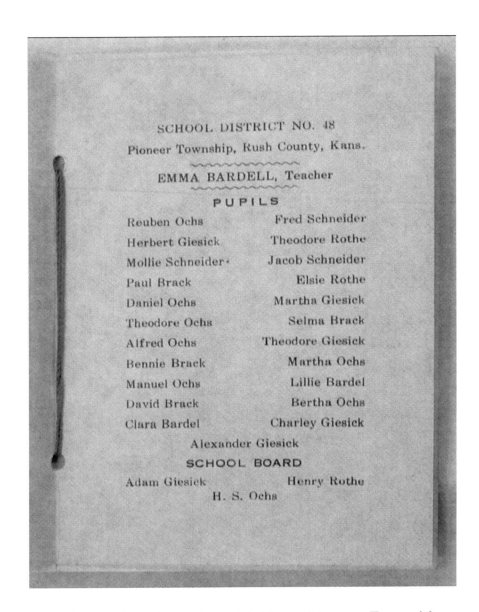

Souvenir School Pamphlet from Pioneer Township, Rush County, Kansas (List of Names)

Note that my grandmother's father, Adam, is on the School Board. Her brothers, Charley and Alex, and her cousins, Theodore and Herbert, are also in attendance. (Birdsong W. J., "Souvenir" - Students/Teachers of School District No. 48, 1912)

Catechism Certificate for Martha Giesick

The Methodist Church of Otis, Kansas presented this Catechism certificate to Martha Giesick on March 31, 1914. (Birdsong W. J., Martha Giesick Catechism certificate from Methodist Church, Otis, Kansas, 1914)

Donald Hergert, in a letter to Grady Birdsong dated September 25, 1988, wrote: *One of the more important documents to come down to us from the Giesick family is the record of marriage, births & deaths. This record, in the hand of Grandfather Adam, (your great-grandfather) dates from c 1905. It currently is in the possession of Verne Giesick, but was lent to me for examination. Its present condition is extremely fragile from handling & folding.* (Hergert, Letter to Grady Birdsong, 1988)

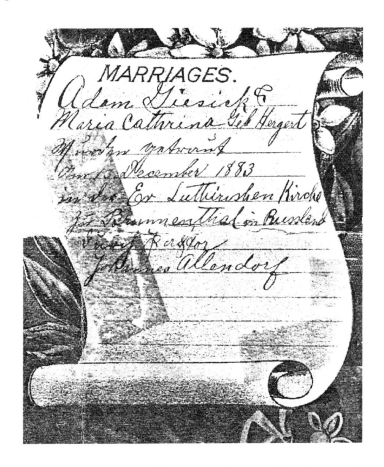

Marriage Certificate of Adam Giesick and Maria Cathrina Gel(born) Hergert

Marriage certificate translated from Russian to English:

Wurden getraut (became married) *um* (on the) 13 December
    1883

In der (in the) *Lutherishen Kirche* (Lutheran Church) *zu* (at)
    Brunnenthal in *Russland* (Russia)

Durch (through or by) Pastor Johannes Allendorf

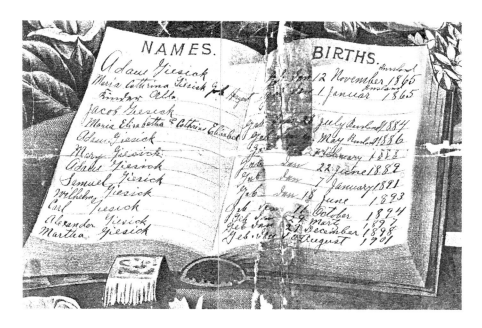

Names of Adam Giesick family recorded in Bible

3rd line ~ *Kinder Alle* (Children all)
Births of Adam Giesick Family recorded in Bible:
'Geb' or Geboren den (born on the) …

Notice Carl Giesick (aka Charlie) is 29 Martz 1897.
*"Grandfather has English phonetics mixed with his
spelling of the German word for the month of March – no T*

and an umlaut over the ä..." (Hergert, Letter to Grady Birdsong, 1988)

Deaths of Adam Giesick family recorded in Bible

However, there is a spot on the page listing births which I could not lift off without lifting the writing so I had to leave it. The date at the area is 6 May 1886 – birthdates of the twins. Occasionally, grandpa would drop letters – as in the case of the 2nd twin, Cathrina Elisabetha. (Hergert, Letter to Grady Birdsong, 1988)

Martha was the youngest of 11 children born to Adam and Maria Kathrina (Hergert) Giesick. Martha's older twin sisters died in 1887, one on June 28 and the other July 15, contrary to what is written in the Family Group Chart. They were born in Brunnental, Russia, and Grandmother Martha told that they were sickly. The trip to America from Russia was very hard for them. As there are no official records, only fragmentary memories of what actually happened and why, we can only imagine the trauma and grief of the family.

The next year another tragedy occurred when an older brother Adam, who was born on February 25, 1888 (noted as 25 May 1888 on Chart) and died the next month, March 9, 1888 (not 1889). Donald verified these corrections in viewing and recording the above writing in the family Bible by Adam, the father of these deceased children. My father has often told the story of his Grandmother Maria (Mary), who wrapped the baby named Adam in a blanket, placed him in the cellar, and walked 14 miles from their sod home to Olmitz, Kansas, to tell husband Adam that their son had passed. Adam worked for a Mr. Brock (the name may have been spelled "Brack"), who lent them a team of horses and wagon to return to bury their young son, who was only days old.

Family Group Chart

HUSBAND'S NAME *Adam Giesick* _____ Nickname _____
When Born: *27 November 1838* Where: *Walter, Russia*
When died: *19 July 1910* Where: *Otis, Kansas*
When married: *b. 1860* Where: _____
Church Affiliation (past) *Ev. Lutheran* (present) *Methodist*
Other wives if any: _____
Separate sheet for ea. mar.
His Father _____ His Mother's Maiden Name _____
Family's Places of Residence: *Walter & Brunnental, Rus. – Bison & Otis, Kans.*
Occupations: Husband: _____ Wife: _____

WIFE'S MAIDEN NAME *Elisabeth Roth* _____ Nickname _____
When born: *19 January 1838* Where: *Walter, Russia*
When died: *15 June 1901* Where: *Otis, Kansas*
Church affiliation (past) *Ev. Lutheran* (present) *Methodist*
Other husbands if any: _____
Separate sheet for ea. mar.
Her Father _____ Her Mother's Maiden Name _____

This information obtained from:
Name: *Donald Hergert*
Address: *4419 Otsego*
City, State, Zip: *Duluth MN 55804*

ANCESTRAL INFORMATION
From where in Germany *origin probably Hess*
From where in Russia *Walter – Brunnental*

Date of immigration *1886*
Name of ship: _____
Port of immigration: _____
Where naturalized _____
Date naturalized _____

M or F		Children (in order of birth)	When Born Day Mo. Yr.	Town Village	Where Born County District	State Country	When Died Day Mo. Yr.	Where Died (& Buried)	Married to	When Married Day Mo. Yr.
M	1	Conrad (Coon)	1862	Brunnental		Rus.	1942	Leoti, Kans.	Anne Catherina Windecker	1880
M	2	Adam	12 Nov 1865	Brunnental		Rus.	1 Sept 1946	Otis, Kans.	Maria Kathrina Hergert	13 Dec 1853
M	3	Wilhelm (Bill)	1868	Brunnental		Rus.	1931	Otis, Kans.	Mary Floessar	c. 189_
	4									
	5									
	6									
	7									
	8									
	9									
	10									
	11									
	12									

AHSGR Form #G-3

Family Group Chart by Donald Hergert

The above Family Group Chart by Donald Hergert documents Grandmother Martha's father Adam (born 12 Nov 1865; died 9 Sept 1946) and his two brothers, Conrad (Coon) and Wilhelm (Bill), who were sons of Adam and Elisabeth (Roth) Giesick of Walter, Russland (Martha's grandfather and grandmother). The family immigrated in 1886.

American Historical Society of Germans From Russia   Family Group Chart

HUSBAND'S NAME *Adam Giesick* _____ Nickname _____

When born: *12 November 1865* Where: *Brunnental, Russia*
When died: *7 September 1946* Where: *Otis, Kansas*
When married: *13 December 1893* Where: *Brunnental, Russia*
Church Affiliation (past) *Ev. Lutheran* (present) *Methodist*
    Buried Otis, Ks. Methodist Cemetery
    (27 Nov 1838 – 14 Jul 1910)   (19 Jan 1838 – 15 Jun 1901)
His Father *Adam Giesick* His Mother's Maiden Name *Elisabeth Roth*
Family's Places of Residence: *Walter and Brunnental, Russia – Otis, Kansas*
Occupations: Husband: *Farmer* Wife: *Housewife*

WIFE'S MAIDEN NAME *Maria Kathrina Hergert* Nickname *Minnie*
When born: *1 January 1865* Where: *Brunnental, Russia*
When died: *9 March 1934* Where: *Otis, Kansas*
Church affiliation (past) *Ev. Lutheran* (present) *Methodist*
    Buried Otis, Ks. Methodist Cemetery
    (23 Feb 1845 – 4 Sept 1917) (17 Sept 1834 – 21 Oct 1906)
Her Father *Jacob Hergert* Her Mother's Maiden Name *Eva Buck*

This information obtained from:
Name: *Donald Hergert*
Address: *4917 Otsego*
City, State, Zip: *Duluth MN 55804*

ANCESTRAL INFORMATION
From where in Germany *Origin probably*
Hessen area
From where in Russia *Walter – Brunnental*

Date of immigration *1886*
Name of ship: _____
Port of immigration: _____
Where naturalized _____
Date naturalized _____

M or F		Children (in order of birth)	When Born Day Mo. Yr.	Town Village	Where Born County District	State Country	When Died Day Mo. Yr.	Where Buried	Married to	When Married Day Mo. Yr.
M	1	Jacob (Jake)	28 Jul 1894	Brunnental, Russia		"	21 Sep 1970	Otis, Kansas	Eva Enos	17 May 1958
F	2	Maria Elisabetha	6 May 1886	"	"	"	15 Jul 1886	Bison, Kansas		
F	3	Kathrina Elisabetha	6 May 1886	"	"	"	15 Jul 1886	"		
M	4	Adam	25 May 1888	Bison	Rush	Ks.	9 Mar 1889	"		
F	5	Mary Katherine	22 Jun 1889	"	"	"	7 Sept 1949	Otis, Kansas	David Hergert	14 Feb 1928
M	6	Adam	7 Jun 1891	Albert	"	"	2 May 1951	Great Bend, Kansas	Mabel Evers	
M	7	Samuel (Sam)	18 Jun 1893	Otis	"	"	22 Feb 1982	Otis, Kansas	Ella Hergert	26 Jun 1949
M	8	Wilhelm (Willie)	14 Oct 1894	"	"	"	20 Jan 1901	"		
M	9	Carl (Charlie)	29 Mar 1897	"	"	"			Elsie Aeis	21 Feb 1922
M	10	Alexander (Alex)	24 Dec 1948	"	"	"	2 Jan 1969	Kans. City, Kansas	Helen Frances Abel	1934
F	11	Martha	10 Aug 1901	"	"	"			Herbert M. Birkney	20 Sep 1924
	12									

AHSGR Form #G-3

Family Group Chart by Donald Hergert (cont. page) (Hergert, Family Group Chart (AHSGR Form #G-3), 1887-1888)

On the church affiliations in Family Group Chart page shown above, the past church affiliation is listed as Evangelical Lutheran, and present is Methodist. Donald Hergert sent to Martha and my parents the article, *"A Lament for Brunnental,"* which had appeared in the German/American newspaper *Die Welt Post* on February 8, 1923. He also wrote the following thoughts accompanied with a poem:

Donald writes: *"... written by Pastor Elias Hergert, a former resident of Brunnental – Have no idea if we are related...?"* He then speculates about the transition of Adam and Maria from Lutheran to the Methodist religion.

I found this an interesting bit of family information and wanted to research it further. The change occurred at a time when the Bolsheviks, under the rule of Lenin, began seizing privately owned land and making it property of the state. This meant that Germans of the lower Volga River colonies, the wealthiest of Russian subjects (as landowners), were having their estates taken away from them. These people were moved from the area; some were deported to Siberia and others were killed. The Bolsheviks invented justifications for these acts.

I found that there were many deliberations and cross-denominational conferencing held by the Catholics, Lutherans, and Mennonites, who were discussing what, should be done about the situation. They decided it best to become a state in early 1918, and pleaded with Lenin to honor their interests. He appeared to consent and created a Soviet Commissariat for the Affairs of the German Volga Colonists. This new circumstance placed them under a stricter governmental control on the local level and fit the Bolshevik agenda of making the goods and lands of the Germans more accessible. In further research, I found this:

With the Bolshevik takeover, the situation in the cities failed to improve. The country was divided in two, with the Red army of the Bolsheviks controlling the Volga and the White army of the old regime controlling 'the other main grain-producing areas of the former Russian Empire—the northern Caucasus, the Kuban, the Don, the Ukraine, and western Siberia'...This created acute Bolshevik dependence on the Volga, not simply for food but for the success of their cause. (Figes, 1989)

The following poem is a lament for the village of Brunnental in the Volga Colonies, calling for all members of the affected family lines (including those living in the United States, South America, and Canada), to unite for a common purpose or agreement. They are not only are being invited to sing this song of sorrow, but also are asked to provide assistance with monetary contributions so that their beloved village can be revived. (This was during the time of the Russian Revolution, when the Bolsheviks were running rampant throughout the countryside.)

A Lament for Brunnental

Oh, Brunnental, how dearly rings
Your name to us from afar.
You are worthy of that which men sing
About you, now (you are) like a dark star.

Once you stood in beautiful splendor,
Your repose was magnificent and great.
Now, who has made you so impoverished?
You've met a most difficult fate.

The hosts of young man, where are they?
Oh old ones, where did they go?
Gone to oblivion, Oh so very early!
And many children also.

You looked for good fortune
Yet it was only a thought.

In your awakening by the Bolsheviks
Horrible is your lot!
You once had strength and riches!
You took your comfort in them.
Now you sit in the dust, so pale,
Just as did Jerusalem!

Jerusalem will again be raised up,
For you my hope does not wane.
In the passing of days and years,
Your splendor will break forth again.

Yet now you seem so afflicted!
Sorrowful as never before!
For Lost are many beautiful homes!
Lost also are many a lofty door!

Oh, mournfully I look on you
As a spirit, you cause me sorrow!
For many a woman and many a man
Have no coat or garment for the morrow.

Tattered, torn, as you are,
I see you as a ghost,
My heart grieves for you!
I weep loudly for those who are lost!

Oh Brunnental, [not readable]
I weep not alone,
For my village comrades here,

135

Their voices are as one.
Now what think all of you,
(Only) a dollar or two
Will help our Brunnental,
Out of its slavery?

Mr. Giesick and Mr. Lebsack, what?
You think, I fight you not,
You went astray in Otis, Kansas,
Here you stand (are placed) in this poem."

Donald continues his writing in 1988: *"Pastor Hergert writes of the conditions in Brunnental (persecutions, murder, and starvation) caused by the raids and confistication of crops and possessions by the Bolsheviks during the revolution, as well as two years of severe drought in this area along the Volga. The poem continues in 100 four-line stanzas that mention many of the farmer residents of Brunnental who then resided in the USA and Canada. He eventually gets around to asking for money to purchase necessities to send to the survivors...*

Imagine my surprise when I came across this verse addressing our grandfather Giesick. Do you know which Mr. Lebsack is mentioned? The "tone" of this stanza suggests there were some hard feelings between Elias Hergert, a Lutheran minister, and these Otis, Kansas residents. Perhaps it is related to leaving the Lutheran Church and becoming Methodists?" (Hergert, Letter to Aunt Martha, 1988)

Volga German Foods

The colonists brought with them many ethnic staple dishes. The mainstay foods were cabbage, uniquely prepared meats, soup, sauerkraut, clabbered milk (sour cream), potatoes, rye bread, cheese, butter, and other assorted nourishments all prepared the old way. *Bierocks* is a scrumptious meal of cabbage, ground beef, bacon, and onions, which is enclosed and baked in bread dough. Offering food to a guest or inviting people for dinner was an important gesture of friendship and politeness among these Volga Germans. This was also my grandmother's way, and she would always have food on hand for guests, family, and friends. You would never go hungry at my grandmother's house!

I had heard and read about the *Der Ova* (German for *oven*) ovens, which were used daily for baking, cooking, and heating. They were made of a mixture of soil and straw, mixed with a small amount of water and baked in the sun. Anything that would burn was used as fuel. Some of the fuels used were dried sunflowers, straw, cow manure, and wood, which was rare on the prairie. The good fuel was called *Mistholz,* and was a compost of barnyard manure that was allowed to ferment naturally in the sun and decompose to a proper consistency. The manure was piled 12 to 20 inches high and mixed with straw. Stock animals were used to walk over and trample this mass until it formed a compact mixture, which would fuel *Der Ova.* It was then cut in squares which would fit in the oven's fire pit or Lehma *Ova* (German for *mud-oven*) fire pit. The fuel would be placed in piles to dry completely before being used.

The walls of these ovens were more than a foot thick. The overall structure was four feet high, three to four feet wide, and about five to six feet in length. During cooking days it was "fired" internally to heat the inside portion, and then the ashes and cinders were removed. The oven would retain its heat for a day of cooking and baking. At the opening was an iron grill that was used for warming coffee pots and fry pans. The area around this oven is where everyone gathered because of the heat generated, especially on cold days.

I am sure that my Great-grandfather and Grandmother Giesick had one of these ovens and used it in the early years of their settlement in Rush County when they arrived in 1886. I know they lived in a sod house (also called *semljanki* or *simolinkas*) when they first came over, according to my Grandmother Martha's many stories of her family and early years on the homestead northwest of Otis, Kansas.

I can remember the many times my Grandmother Martha baked. As small children, my younger sister Rhea and I would hover around the kitchen table for the leftover goodies. One of our favorites was leftover pie dough rolled flat, sprinkled with sugar and cinnamon, and baked to perfection. That was the highlight of any day when grandmother was baking in her kitchen. We also reveled in the leftover cookie dough (which wasn't a lot when grandmother was done putting the cookie dough in the oven), but at that time it seemed like huge mountains of delight to us sugar-craving little children. (Birdsong G. T., Martha Birdsong Homemaker, 1901-1993)

Unity and Tradition on the Prairie

I often try to imagine what it must have been like for Adam (the junior), his father Adam (the senior), and their families to settle in this new region. I have relied heavily on other narratives of documented stories of the Volga-Germans that came to this area. There are very few family stories of the early days of arrival of my great-grandparents in Rush County. The few documented stories of others will have to suffice, coupled with the imagination to envision what our ancestor's new venture was like. One thing that stands out is that these Volga-Germans came as a family unit or in groups that had lived together in the Volga colonies and knew one another. However, Rush County Historians Schneider and Haning, in Chapter XXII of their book, *Rush County Kansas,* capture further rituals, routines, traditions, and daily tasks of these hearty people. These women obviously were of the German-Volga ancestry to provide the following insights:

This outline of German-Russian life style enables the present-day reader to understand how these settlers came as a group of old acquaintances who started again in a country very reminiscent of their home land, who carried on their traditions, spoke their home language, clung to their traditions, and only gradually grew into American styles. For about ten years they farmed, went to church, brought in necessary supplies by wagon and team. Prior to 1886 Olney, Scheuerman, Belfield, and Schoental were recognized as Post Offices or community names. The nearest railroads had been at Larned, Great Bend, or Hays. Supplies were freighted in by teams in about a day's trip. At first there were no schools or church buildings. These came after homes and fields of grain were established. People traveled by wagons drawn by horse or oxen, horseback or sometimes by buggy. There had been early Indian scares but Indians were no real menace after the first settlement and after 1878 there were even no friendly visitations by Indians. Old timers recalled uncomfortable things such as prairie fires, snakes, scarcity of rain [Global Warming was not yet a laughing matter ☺], *shortage of crops, lonesomeness, and blizzards. Good times were experienced in literarys, spelling bees, quilting bees, and church gatherings in schoolhouses or homes.*

...The German Lutheran Church was organized in 1877 by 47 German families of the Schoental community. In later years this church disintegrated into the Lutheran Methodist and Baptist churches in Otis and Bison.

...1886 would seem a year of unbelievable railroad expansion. In fact the Great Bend Tribune of December 3, 1886 remarked that, "The number of railroads under construction to every little town in Western Kansas is only equaled by the number of street railways, waterworks, electric lights, colleges and children to fill them. A town of 150 inhabitants that hasn't had at least 4 trunk lines and all these other advantages is considered too unimportant to put on the maps.

...To get rail service local communities would vote bonds to finance the railroads coming. (Haning, 1976)

You could liken this growth and expansion to today's trucking and airline industries and the routing that they have provided over the course of the last 90 to 100 years. The airline pricing models have conformed to population markets throughout the entire world, and, of course, we have seen the various airlines (such as Trans World Airways, Pan Am, and TWA) who were competing for traveler dollars, appear and vanish. Likewise, the trucking and shipping industries have proliferated, with Federal Express and UPS as the current main competitors for shipment of goods. I surmise this was also the case with the railroads in the late 1800s and early 1900s, which performed transport of both goods and people.

In the early days, post offices came and went with amazing speed. Scheuerman, Olney and Belfield disappeared. Otis had a post office by 1888. The man who built the first post office building (he is thought to have been Avery Avis) made it large enough to accommodate a general store as well. In keeping with their Russian heritage, farmers set up small businesses in the town at the same time maintaining their farms they had held for ten or twelve years...

In 1889 the Schoental Lutherans moved their church to Otis. The first church in Otis was a 20 x 30 stone building on the site of the present church. The attic of the church doubled as a temporary parsonage... In 1894 certain families pulled from the Lutheran Church to organize the Emmanuel German Methodist Church. Their new building was built in 1895. Its distinctive antique architecture remains a useful and quite functional landmark of the city. (Haning, 1976)

The 1890s were hard years for our ancestors. The scant census information in the 1900 census reveals very little about the times for the Giesick family and others. A mental picture of these times is just now unfolding.

The 1890s were busy years, with many immigrants coming to join families and friends or to make new settlements. Poor crop years would drive the disheartened away. Good crop years would yield enough to pay for land and brighten prospects for more. Wheat was 40¢ per bushel in 1893. Times were hard; banks failed. People kept their money in old teapots; fruit jars, and socks. (Haning, 1976)

I can remember Grandma Martha telling stories of the saving of hard currency (coins) and greenbacks (dollars). People would hide their money in various places around their houses or property; the money might turn up after they had passed, being discovered in places such as mattresses, attic, or in plastered walls or old coffee cans hidden away.

Locusts struck from 1876 through 1893 too frequently for comfort. As late as 1894, J. P. Pomeroy, a millionaire land promoter, was still going to Russia to encourage immigration. Those who stuck it out through thick and thin began to prosper. By the 1912-1913 years certain families had come to sufficient wealth that the younger generation could have the finest in... (Haning, 1976)

In researching all of the area census data, I found Adam and Elisabeth (Roth) Giesick in the Twelfth Census of the United States, enumerated in June of 1900. Adam and Elisabeth are the parents of Conrad, Adam, and Wilhelm. Adam is the middle son is Grandmother Martha's father. For clarity, I will refer to him as Adam (the junior) and his father as Adam (the senior). The census shows Adam (the senior) and Elisabeth being born in 1838 in Russia.

Additional records specify that both were born in Walter, Russia. This census notates their age as being 62 years of age and that a son, William (32 years old), his wife Meary (probably *Mary* misspelled) and their son Henry (2 years old) as living with them. It also spells the last name as *Gisick*, which explains why it does not come up readily in the census data when queried for the spelling of Giesick. The township (abbreviated TWP) is Pioneer Township in Rush County, Kansas.

(Government U. S., Kansas Decennial Census, 1915)

Column 16 of the census forms is for the year of immigration, which is marked "1887" for Adam, Elisabeth, and William. Column 17 asks how many years they have been residing in the United States, and is marked "12 years." Column 18 is marked "NAT," which indicates that Adam, Elisabeth, and William are all naturalized citizens of the United States. Column 19 shows the occupation as "farmer" in Adam's case and "farm laborer" for William. The last four columns, 25 to 28, deal with ownership, farm ground, and equipment:

Column 25 - Owned or Rented = "O" for Owned
Column 26 - Owed; Free of Mortgage = "F" for Mortgage-free
Column 27 - Farm House - F (meaning there is a house on property)
Column 28 - Number of Farm Schedule = 48 *

* Agriculture schedules were recorded starting in 1840 through the 1910 censuses. They contained a great amount of data about the specific farm. Typically, it would include the name of the owner of the farm, how long he had farmed that land, acreage, the value of the farm, expenses to operate the farm, the type and value of the farm produce, and the quantity of livestock, if any. Other information, such as the amount of the specific crop, what was produced yearly, and the amount of acreage it took to produce that crop, was available. The 1890 schedules were, for the most part, destroyed by fire, leaving only a few states with this census

data. The 1900 and 1910 schedules were ordered destroyed by Congress.

Adam Giesick ~ Grandmother Martha's brother, born June 7, 1891. (Birdsong W. J., Photo of Adam Giesick, Early 1900s)

In the next census of 1910, Adam (the junior) reflects almost the same data logged on the 1900 census, with the exception that he showed a mortgage on the grounds and house. Mortgages are the price of doing business or engaging in any farming venture. This suggests that Grandfather Adam was a forward-thinking businessman and farmer, doing all the risk assessments involved with farming—and betting on the odds.

All bets were placed on wheat in Kansas during the upsurge of immigration in the late 1800 and early 1900s. It was the lifeblood of many who settled this land.

I found the following historical data on wheat on an Oklahoma State Department of Education website:

History of Wheat

Domestic wheat originated in southwest Asia in what is now known as the Fertile Crescent. The oldest archaeological evidence for wheat cultivation comes from Syria, Jordan, Turkey, Armenia, and Iraq. Around 9000 years ago, wild einkorn wheat was harvested and domesticated in the first archaeological signs of sedentary farming in the Fertile Crescent. Wild einkorn wheat still grows in the Fertile Crescent.

Around 8,000 years ago, a mutation or hybridization occurred within emmer wheat, resulting in a plant with seeds that were larger but could not sow themselves on the wind. While this plant could not have succeeded in the wild, it produced more food for humans. In cultivated fields this plant outcompeted plants with smaller, self-sowing seeds and become the primary ancestor of modern wheat breeds.

Columbus packed wheat on his ships on his second voyage to the New World.

While wheat was grown in the United States during the early colonial years, it was not until the late 19th century that wheat cultivation flourished, owing to the importation of an especially hardy strain of wheat known as Turkey red wheat. Russian immigrants who settled in Kansas brought Turkey red wheat with them.

Wheat is well adapted to harsh environments and is mostly grown on wind-swept areas too dry and too cold for rice and corn.

Wheat supplies about 20 percent of the food calories for the world's people and is a national staple in many countries. In Eastern Europe and Russia, over 30 percent of the calories consumed come from wheat. About one third of the world's people depend on wheat for their nourishment.

The per capita consumption of wheat in the United States exceeds that of any other single food staple. (http://Oklahoma4h.okstate.edu, 2010)

Imagine the incentive these immigrants felt when they laid eyes upon the prairie lands of the sweeping steppes of Kansas. They brought with them many years of expertise and knowhow, readily adapting to the work of building communities, churches, lives, a new culture, and cottage industries in this inhospitable environment.

From the Kansas State Historical Society website: As early as 1888, people were proclaiming Kansas the wheat state. *"All parts of Kansas grow good corn but in wheat, Kansas can beat the world," Topeka Daily Capital*, 1888. In 1949, Kansas license plates came out with *"The Wheat*

State" stamped on them. I was four years old at the time. I remember seeing the plates when I was young and thinking it was quite natural that wheat was here before humans came to this land. Of course, I didn't yet know the whole story!

In my research, I came across this interesting perspective by a history professor at Kansas University. He seems to have focused upon the importance of the crop and its value to humankind. I would like to note that, though this was written a generation ago (in 1944); I believe it still has relevance to humanity and food sources in today's and tomorrow's society. This observation also highlights our family's small-but-important contribution during these times. In addition, we can look to the successes and prosperity which the Giesick families achieved in the late 1800 and early 1900s in the wheat fields of Rush County.

The bread-eating civilization and the rice-eating civilization have largely divided the world between them, and the rice-eaters have been rapidly becoming bread-eaters. Wheat has been becoming of increasing importance to the twentieth-century world. High-gluten wheat's are the best bread wheat, and as Carleton so often pointed out, aridity and high gluten quality seem to be inseparable. As far as the North American continent is concerned, the Plains region, which produces hard spring and winter wheat, is the only source of supply of such wheat. Instead of abandonment, the long-time demands of the world for bread would seem to call for more effective utilization of sub-humid areas, not only of this continent, but of others. A large part of the meat supply of the continent is derived also from the sub-humid grass lands as breeding grounds, and these are linked in a regional interdependency, as in the case of the Southwestern Great Plains. (Malin, 1944)

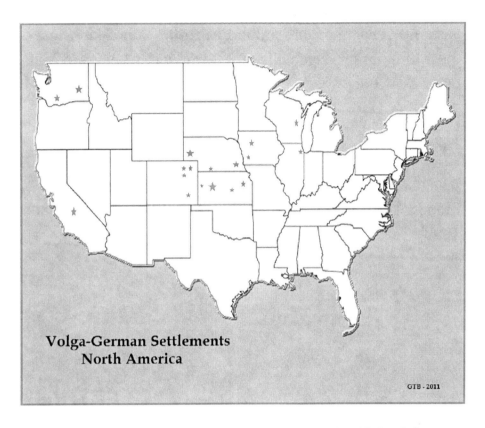

Map of Volga-German Settlements in the United States

The above map of the USA gives the reader a general idea of where Volga-German colonists settled in North America. My research led me to create this map by notating each general area of settlement. Please note the center of America, the Kansas area, where the following counties had significant populations of Volga Germans: Ellis, Russell, Rush, Barton, Ness, Trego, and Wichita counties. Colorado had significant numbers of Germans settle in Weld, La

Salle, and Larimer counties in the northeast section of the state. Nebraska had small to medium populations in the Scottsbluff and Gering area as well as McCook, and in the eastern part of the state around Lincoln, Nebraska. Most of these immigrants specialized in growing wheat and sugar beets early on.

Family Group Chart

Adam and Maria Kathrina (Hergert) Giesick Family
Pioneer TWP (Township), Rush County, Otis, Kansas 1800-1900's

Husband	Adam Giesick	
Birth	Nov. 12, 1865	Brunnental, Russia
Marriage	Dec. 13, 1883	Brunnental, Russia
Death	Sep. 7, 1946	Otis, Kansas
Burial		
Other Wives		
Parents		

Wife	Maria Kathrina Giesick [Hergert]	
Birth	Jan. 1, 1865	Brunnental, Russia
Death	Mar. 9, 1934	Otis, Kansas
Burial		
Other Husbands		
Parents		

Children

1	Jacob "Jake" Giesick	
Gender	Male	
Birth	Jul. 28, 1884	Brunnental, Russia
Wife	**Eva Giesick [Foos]**	
Marriage	Mar. 17, 1908	
Death	Sep. 21, 1970	Otis, Kansas
Burial		Otis, Kansas

2	Maria Elisabetha Giesick	
Gender	Female	
Birth	May 6, 1886	Brunnental, Russia
Husband		
Marriage		
Death	Jun. 28, 1887	Bison, Kansas
Burial		Bison, Kansas

151

3	Kathrina Elisabetha Giesick	
Gender	Female	
Birth	May 6, 1886	Brunnental, Russia
Husband		
Marriage		
Death	Jul. 15, 1887	Bison, Kansas
Burial		Bison, Kansas

4	Adam Giesick	
Gender	Male	
Birth	Feb. 25, 1888	Bison, Kansas
Wife		
Marriage		
Death	Mar. 9, 1888	Bison, Kansas
Burial		Bison, Kansas

5	Mary Katherine Hergert [Giesick]	
Gender	Female	
Birth	Jun. 22, 1889	Bison, Kansas
Husband	David Hergert	
Marriage	Feb. 14, 1908	
Death	Sep. 7, 1947	Otis, Kansas
Burial		Otis, Kansas

6	Adam Giesick	
Gender	Male	
Birth	Jun. 7, 1891	Albert, Kansas
Wife	Mabel Giesick [Evers]	
Marriage		
Death	May 2, 1951	Great Bend, Kansas
Burial		Great Bend, Kansas

7	Samuel "Sam" Giesick	
Gender	Male	
Birth	Jun. 18, 1893	Otis, Kansas
Wife	Ella Giesick [Hergert]	
Marriage	Jun. 26, 1919	
Death	Feb. 22, 1982	Otis, Kansas
Burial		Otis, Kansas

8	Wilhelm "Willie" Giesick	
Gender	Male	
Birth	Oct. 11, 1894	Otis, Kansas
Wife		
Marriage		
Death	Jan. 20, 1901	Otis, Kansas
Burial		Otis, Kansas

9	Carl "Charley" Giesick	
Gender	Male	
Birth	Mar. 29, 1897	Otis, Kansas
Wife	Elsie Giesick [Avis]	
Marriage	Feb. 21, 1922	
Death		Otis, Kansas
Burial		Otis, Kansas

10	Alexander "Alex" Giesick	
Gender	Male	
Birth	Dec. 29, 1898	Otis, Kansas
Wife	Helen Frances Giesick [Abel]	
Marriage	1934	
Death	Jan. 2, 1967	Kansas City, Kansas
Burial		Kansas City, Kansas

11	Martha Birdsong [Giesick]	
Gender	Female	
Birth	Aug. 10, 1901	Otis, Kansas
Husband	Herbert Monroe Birdsong	
Marriage	Sep. 20, 1922	Ellsworth, KS
Death	Nov. 29, 1993	Denver, Colorado
Burial		Hoisington, Kansas

Family Group Chart by Grady T. Birdsong and Donald Hergert (Birdsong G. T., Family Group Chart, 1887-1888)

I have reproduced this data from Donald Hergert's original research and keyed this chart from his first family group chart with the updated information on the family.

I have many fond memories of visiting Grandmother's brother's farms (Samuel and Charley Giesick). It is the original homestead. My father, "Seedy" (H. M. Birdsong), had a special bond with his Uncle Sam and Uncle Charley, and we visited them quite often, hunting pheasants and rabbits. My father helped his uncles during the harvests almost every summer when he was a young man. When we visited the farms, we usually would hunt some game and bring it home for Grandmother to prepare a family meal. We looked forward to sitting down to a meal of oven-baked pheasant or fried cottontail rabbit, which Grandmother prepared so adeptly. She learned these skills from her Volga German mother and father.

Samuel Giesick took over the family homestead land four miles east and one mile north of Otis, Kansas, from his father, and lived in the house (pictured below) that had been built in 1892.

Hiram M. (Seedy) Birdsong in front yard of the Giesick homestead near Otis, Kansas. Herbert M. and Martha are in background. (Birdsong W. J., Photo Uncle Sam Giesick Farmhouse, 1924-25)

I remember, as a young child, visiting the homestead farm. Aunt Ella would catch a chicken, wring its neck, and prepare fried chicken with mashed potatoes, gravy, corn, canned vegetables (in Ball® jars), pickles, and all the trimmings. We children always looked forward to Aunt Ella's meals.

Giesick Farmhouse March 1987 (Birdsong W. J., Photo of Uncle Sam Giesick Farmhouse, 1987)

Giesick Farm Outbuildings, 1987 (Birdsong W. J., Photo of Uncle Sam Giesick Barn and Windmill, 1987)

Ella Giesick, Samuel's wife (Birdsong W. J., Photograph of Ella Giesick, Early 1900s)

My father remembers his family spending time with his grandparents at the homestead west and north of Otis. They would spend many hours on the farm and had access to a pony. Riding this pony was great fun, and they would delight in putting this animal through the paces during their many hours of playtime around the farm. One time, during a visit to the grandparents' farm, little brother Bob was riding the pony and it became tired of being ridden. When the pony got near the stock tank, it bolted to the trough and lowered its head, pitching Bob headfirst into the tank. Hearing all the wailing and thrashing in the water, Grandfather Adam came upon the scene, immediately thought that Dad was the culprit, and was about to paddle his butt when his mother Martha came to the rescue and toned down the situation. My father told me that it was a case of mistaken identity and that he was always respectful and mindful of his Grandfather Adam (the junior) because he had learned very early on he was a no-nonsense fellow.

Great-grandfather Adam was a firm but fair man, according to my father. He was raised in the Lutheran ways and baptized into the church in Russia, but became interested in the Methodist doctrine upon immigrating to Rush County. He became very active in both the building and administering of the first Otis, Kansas Methodist church (shown below) in the early 1900s and was a charter member. Grandfather Adam held many offices and positions of leadership in the church, ranging from superintendent, to member of Board of Trustees and Board of Stewards, to becoming a licensed lay preacher. Most of the people who migrated to this area from Russia were members of the Lutheran or Reformed Church. This nucleus of people started meeting in the area schoolhouse or town stores for their church services without a regular preacher. This humble beginning in Rush County, northwest of Bison, became known as a German Methodist country church. In 1894, this congregation was organized into the Emmanuel German Methodist Church. The church was completed and dedicated on December 22, 1895. The first Board of Trustees included my Great-grandfather Adam.

Another family story passed down verbally to my father by his cousin, Donald Hergert, begins with Great-grandmother Mary Kathrine (Hergert) and Great-grandfather Adam (the junior) being married in Russia, December 13, 1883, three years before coming to America. Reportedly, Mary stayed behind in Russia for five months before following her husband Adam to Rush County, Kansas. According to their grandson Donald Hergert, Grandmother Mary used her sister's passport and smuggled her twins out of Russia by hiding them between pillows. Her oldest son Jacob and his aunt were also spirited through immigrations under cover. The two disappeared for a couple of days and were reunited with Jacob's mother Mary after a brief time. The details of what actually happened in their disappearance have been lost in time.

Great-Grandfather Adam (the junior) and his wife Mary eventually settled and homesteaded the ground four miles west and one mile north. They built the farmhouse shown above in 1892 and lived there until 1917, when they moved into the town of Otis proper. Samuel (the younger) then took over this original dwelling and that quarter of ground. (Birdsong H. M., 2010)

Methodist Church, Otis, Kansas, 2010
(Photo by Author)

My great grandparents are buried in the Otis, Kansas, cemetery, as is most of the rest of the family. Grandmother Martha, I am told by my father, helped prepare (embalm) my Great-grandmother Mary on the kitchen table in their home prior to her burial in March 1934. From an early age, I sensed that my Grandmother was totally prepared for any of life's traumas that might come her way. She tacitly passed on that preparedness to me through her son, and I thank her for this to this day. I did not know it yet in childhood, but she was one of a few who prepared me for the rigors of Vietnam.

Chapter 5 ~ A World War Comes to Kansas

The Call to Duty

Not many of our immediate family were involved in "the war to end all wars"— World War I. Grandfather's brother, James Christian, served in the U.S. Navy during that time, and our Great-uncle Samuel Giesick, my Grandmother Martha's brother, was called to serve our country in mid-1917, at the beginning of WWI. He first registered for the draft on June 5, 1917, as was notated on his draft registration card, which I obtained from the National Archives. I also found his brother's draft card and registration, but Great-uncle Carl (called *Charlie*) was not called to service. I suspect he was a Classification II, which meant that he was exempt in the first round of inductees and probably deemed essential to carry on with farm work.

Samuel was destined to honorably serve with Company C of the 137th Infantry, 69th Brigade within the 35th Infantry Division (Santa Fe Division, named after the Santa Fe Trail from Kansas to New Mexico) from initial induction in September 1917 through May 11, 1919, when he was discharged (US Army, 1919). This division was formed into an active duty unit in July 1917. It was one of the 17 National Guard divisions brought into active service during World War I from around the United States. Some elements of this unit began forming at Camp Funston, close to Junction City, Kansas (present-day Fort Riley, Kansas).

I found an interesting history of this division, titled *Heroes of the Argonne* by Charles B. Hoyt, written in 1919 shortly after the hostilities were terminated in Europe. It mentions that the sense of urgency felt throughout America was not quickly established in the beginning, upon the anticipation and declaration of war in Europe. That is one man's opinion. In the chapter, "The Rookie Days," the following mental picture of buildup gives us an idea of what was transpiring at the time:

The National Guard troops were not called as quickly as anticipated, and a breathing space for recruiting and organizing was offered by the delay. August 5 the troops of the two states (Kansas and Missouri) were called out and assigned to home camps, where an initial baptism of hikes and drills began. Steadily from then until October, when the mobilization was complete, a stream of guard troops flowed toward Camp Doniphan. Here organizations were allotted designated areas and entered on an intensive program of exercises, marches and drills, and an extensive daily menu of Oklahoma dust. (Hoyt, 1919)

Samuel sent a postcard to his sister Martha from Camp Funston in September 1917, expressing his newfound awe for the military. He writes:

*This is Sunday but we don't notice it here much, though [it] seems to be a real nice day but as far as we can see is nothing but barracks in every direction. I have not been very far since I been here but it is a big place... [Not legible] *%# Co 4 Batts 164 Depot Brigate, Camp Funston, Kansas.*

Below is the front of that postcard, which was saved by my mother, W. J. Birdsong.

**Camp Funston, Kansas Induction Process, 1917
(Birdsong W. J., Post Card of Camp Funston, Kansas
Induction Process, 1917)**

Most of the division started organizing *stand to* (an Army term for *organizing*) operations and training exercises in August of that year at Camp Doniphan, Oklahoma (today it is Fort Sill, Lawton, Oklahoma). The targeted headcount for the nucleus of this division was taken from the states of Kansas and Missouri. This division was made up of three machine gun battalions, three field artillery regiments, four infantry regiments, one combat engineering regiment, and a signaling battalion that had a total potential Table of Organization of over 26,000 men.

Following is another typical WWI type of postcard, passed on to me by my mother (Mrs. H. M. Birdsong), which was originally sent to Mr. Adam Giesick in Otis, Kansas, on March 7, 1918, by his son Samuel during training at Camp Doniphan near Lawton, Oklahoma. The writing on the back states:

Rec'd your kind letter and going out early in the morning on a 6 day hike so you might not hear from me for a few days till we get back again. Just wanted to let you know so don't worry. –Your loving son, Samuel

This message seems to convey the urgency of the training, but at the same time, my great-uncle is trying to assuage his parents' fears when he naively knows the gravity of his training and that he soon will be in harm's way.

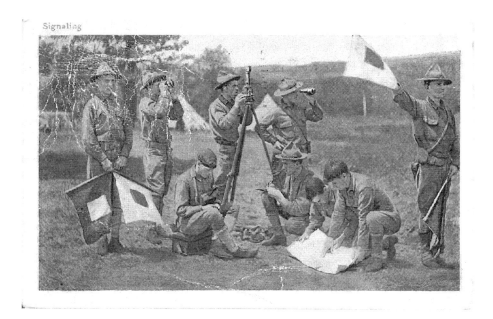

Semaphore Signaling Exercises - Camp Doniphan, Oklahoma, 1918 (Birdsong W. J., Post Card of Semaphore Signaling Exercises - Camp Doniphan, Oklahoma, 1918)

In my examination of the available history of this unit, I came across a paper written in 1953, which is archived in the United States Army War College and Carlisle Barracks in Carlisle, Pennsylvania. In this history, I found some interesting regional customs that will give the reader an idea about young men leaving their homes in wartime and going abroad and how they are perceived in other locales. Troops traveling through areas other than their own typically stand out. Locals perceive in many different ways and often assign stigmas. These men were looked upon with suspicion due to the then-popular dime novels depicting cowboys, Indians, and the Wild West. The medium's written reputations preceded these desperate creatures from Kansas and Missouri.

The winter of 1917 was a severe winter on the high plains of Kansas, Oklahoma, and Nebraska. This was, in essence, a good thing. Although it was brutal, the winter prepared these troops for the hardships they would endure in France in the coming months.

Upon arriving in New York City to prepare for their transport by sea to Europe, the men of the Santa Fe Division attracted much attention because each wore an issued campaign hat (known nowadays as a "Smokey Bear hat") with a conventional cavalryman's chin strap. Wind on the high plains made the chin strap a necessity for keeping the government-provided head and shade protection on their heads. Hence, they became known in the New York press as the *"Chin Strap Division from the West"* and the *"Cowboy Division."* It was known throughout the New York metropolitan area that these young men were cowpunchers, ranchers, and farmers. (Department of the Army, 1953)

On April 25th, the 137th Infantry left Camp Mills on Long Island and boarded the transport ship Karmala. Companies A, B, and C, were assigned to the Karmala. My great-uncle was a member of Company C. Clearing and registering through the customs house, they received tickets to determine bunk area, mess area, and lifeboat assignments. The assorted transports in the convoy involved with ferrying the 35th Division were the Baltic, Karmala, Aeneas, Carona, Teutonic, and Adriatic, all under escort by a large cruiser.

Excitement precedes the embarkation stage of the war process. This exhilaration is keenly captured in the history book, *Reminiscences of the 137th U.S. Infantry* by Carl Haterius. He writes:

As we filed over the gangplank, the cheering was lacking, but the thrill was there. Although we felt and realized the parting meant [being] away from home, friends and country, no one knew for how long, still, as we crossed that gang-plank and stepped aboard those huge monsters of the deep there was a certain feeling of adventure about it all which more or less appealed to us. We were desirous to know what the future held in store, and as young-spirited disciples, we craved not a little excitement. No sooner were we on board than such remarks as, "Hope we see some submarines on this trip; like to see what they look like!" were heard. That is the American Yank every time. No matter how great the danger or excitement, he wants to be right there. (Haterius, 1919)

The convoy arrived in England on May 7, 1917, resupplied, and went on to Le Havre, France, where the soldiers disembarked and boarded trains for northeast France and the Western Front. It was here that the doughboys were introduced to the "Forty and Eight" boxcars. The narrow-gauge railroads of France employed these boxcars, which carried about half the capacity of American Pullman boxcars. Each boxcar carried 40 men or 8 horses, or a combination of the two. Memories of riding in these boxcars are still vivid: rickety, unheated, rough riding, long, slow trips, came to the minds of this fraternity of men who were confined to these rail cars on their journeys to the front.

In June 1918, elements of the Santa Fe Division moved into position in the southeast portion of the Western Front near Epinal, France. It was in this area that the 35th Infantry Division started engaging the Germans in minor skirmishes. Repositioning to Blainville for re-staging, point elements of the Division night-marched to the heavily wooded area of Nancy and originated the first major American offensive toward St. Michiel. The overall push into German-held territory was at a cost of over 7,000 casualties, mostly light wounds. The doughboys of the 35th Division captured an estimated 16,000 German prisoners and over 400 artillery pieces.

A few days later, the 137th and 138th Infantry Regiments of the 35th Division started toward the Argonne forest to prepare for the big offensive that was being planned for the Meuse-Argonne area on that Western Front in September. On September 26, the 35th Division launched a savage attack into the German lines. The 137th in the lead (on point) was assigned the sector, which featured the dreaded Vauquois Hill. This edifice, a butte-like fortress, appeared impregnable and was unobtainable by the French in earlier battles.

The 137th Infantry was designated the lead regiment and were, according to the French, used as the sacrificial unit to take this Boche (German) stronghold. During the beginning of this offensive, they were met by heavy German resistance. The division suffered so many casualties that it finally was pulled back, placed into a reserve status, and told to "stand down" (an Army term for *reorganizing*).

According to the 137th Infantry history paper I obtained from the U.S. Army Heritage & Education Center, *The 137th in five days of action had taken every assigned objective but had suffered extremely heavy losses with 107 killed, 38 dead of wounds, 1,060 wounded, and 88 listed as prisoners or missing. This represented 46% of the men engaged, and the Regiment withdrew to the Argonne area for a well-earned rest.* (Department of the Army, 1953)

I read about the gains of this campaign and learned that a total of about six miles of ground was taken around the area north of Exermont, France, by this unit. This movement into enemy territory and the capture of over 900, including 12 officers, later was considered an acceptable gain. A considerable amount of German artillery pieces also were captured and removed from the battlefield.

The 35th Division moved again and was positioned into a line sector close to Verdun. It was rumored that an armistice was in the making, and occasionally the men would obtain a worn copy of a foreign edition of the daily papers. Gossip from these rag sheets traveled at lightning speed among the troops, relieving the boredom and brightening up a dismal day of continuous rain, knee-deep water, and trench mud.

The men crafted visions of their familiar world and longed to go back to their seemingly delightful prior existence. It was at this time, and amongst these daydreams and gossip, that the 81st Division, also known as the Wildcat Division, relieved the regiment in the trenches. Haterius points out: *The great majority of the men in the relieving division were new at the game of war, having seen very little training and no direct participation in any battle. It was their first trip to the trenches. As the relief was being effected, some amusing incidents took place. Our boys, knowing their newly arrived comrades were "rookies" at the game, took every possible advantage of the fact (You can't beat a doughboy). One of our men, noticing the relief coming up, approached and enquired, "What organization is this?" The reply, "The 81st Division; they call us the Wildcats. What do they call you?" The husky Kansan replied, "They didn't have to call us; we volunteered.*" Both parties appreciated the joke. (Haterius, 1919)

The 81st Division Wildcats was a unit that came from North and South Carolina and the Florida area. They would later be tested on the front lines of Verdun and suffered heavy causalities before the armistice.

This war was unique in that it was fought for territory, and the methods and tactics used were innovative and manpower-intensive. *"The trenches in which the infantry found it kept no uniform distance from that of the Germans. Each system of earthworks, both ours and that of the enemy, twisted and serpentined over the hills... The trenches were deep enough to shelter an infantryman from the enemy gaze without need of his bending or crouching."* (Hoyt, 1919)

These methods and tactics changed when the units of the 35th Division found themselves in the forest areas of the Western Front.

To give the reader an idea about daily troop living conditions, I will share the following passage from the Haterius book: *"While here at Le Bresse (Alsace), the regiment was given its first 'cootie baths,' which no doubt sounds interesting. Previous to our arrival in France, we had often read of how the soldiers had to combat trench vermin, which, broadly speaking, meant dog-sized rats, cooties, and a certain disease known as trench itch. We were now experiencing some of this... Rats, almost dog-sized, long hairy, spring-tailed brutes.. Their favorite dish happened to be the lobe of the ear... Our little friend, the 'cootie,' is strictly a species of body lice, and is known as a blood sucker. The more one scratches, the faster they creep... The only means of ridding your clothes of them is to treat your garments to a dry steam bath."* (Haterius, 1919)

I personally know of this phenomenon, having spent two tours in the hedgerows, rice paddies, jungle, rain, and mud of Vietnam in 1968 and 1969.

Even though my great-uncle would not talk about the war much, my father told me one story that his Uncle Sam had told him about the war and his extremely hard time in the Argonne. Keep in mind my great-uncle Sam spoke not only English but also very good German, having learned it from his father and mother as a youngster, and he used this vernacular in the daily transactions of life in and around the towns and townships of central Kansas.

Here is the story: The offensive had begun, and on this day of extreme fighting and meeting with heavy resistance from the German army, an American drive was halted and the men of the line company were regrouping and staging for another assault. The battle lines and trenches were so close to each other that you could hear the Germans talking to each other, according to Uncle Sam. His platoon commander heard some Germans calling out to each other as though they were either lost or confused and asked Sam to listen and see what they were talking about. It so happened that they were separated from their unit and seemed lost as he translated their conversation in German.

The platoon commander, in discussing the situation with Uncle Sam, asked him if he thought he could talk them into the doughboy lines to capture them. Uncle Sam was reluctant at first and then decided he would give it a try, but stipulated that there was no guarantee that he could do it. He then moved quickly outside the front lines with his 1911A-1 .45 caliber government issued pistol and maneuvered close to where the Germans were talking to each other. Moving into place as best he could and locking and loading his sidearm, Uncle Sam began softly whistling and calling to them in German the equivalent of "over here." In a short time, one German walked out from behind a large tree in the forest at what is known in military circles and on the parade field as the "port arms" (a rifle held at a 45-degree angle with both hands in front of one's chest) ready position. Uncle Sam had already mentally anticipated a "fire fight" situation and was aiming his cocked field pistol at the man when he appeared right in front of him. Uncle Sam admitted to my father that he was frightened, but he tried to remain visibly calm while he coaxed the German to put down his rifle.

The German surrendered right away, lay down his rifle, and called for his two other compatriots to come to where he and Uncle Sam were positioned. They both eagerly came right away. Sam then guided the three of them into the American position and arranged to feed them and interrogate them for any useful intelligence.

It turns out that the German soldiers were worn to a frazzle, hungry, tired, and scared; they were at the low ebb of existence. Uncle Sam told my father that he was amazed that they were just like the men of the American army and had the same needs for food, warmth, security, and vigilance of what was going on around them. After conversing with them in German, he found that they were God-fearing, family-oriented men who were discouraged at their losses, the daily combat in the trenches, being in the forest, and lacking leadership. Their morale appeared to be extremely low, according to our Uncle Sam.

Those that have experienced combat are aware that there comes with it a constant fatigue and total exhaustion of the body that overcomes you but does not totally strip away your basic instincts, functions or senses to survive. Though it takes a toll on your psyche and energy, you remain in a dull, constant state of vigilance of your surroundings and mission. Sometimes the need for sleep overrides all else, and you succumb unwillingly to that basic need. It is only human, unless you are scared out of your mind or have experienced an abundant surge of adrenaline. This probably was the case that night for my Uncle Sam, as he guarded the German prisoners and unwillingly fell asleep. He was later startled awake by one of the prisoners who had taken it upon himself to place a trench coat over Sam to keep him warm. The soldier's act of kindness was a revelation to my uncle, one that stayed with him for years afterward. When he related the story to my father, he was still in awe of those German prisoners and their humanity. He told my father that they were just like Americans and wanted the same things: security, happiness, family, liberty and the like. I have heard this story a few times from my father in our private conversations when he spoke about his uncles and their influence on him.

In Hoyt's book, a mental picture of the fatigue that our soldiers endured is vividly portrayed: *"The Soldier tired enough knows no bed more comfortable than one of French mud. On their initiation into night hikes, they believed they would never accustom themselves to sleeping in it. The early stages of night marching convinced them to the contrary. Officers and men alike would stretch themselves in the slime to snatch a brief respite. The water soaking through their already rain- and sweat-soaked clothing, they would fall asleep almost instantly with a calmness that civilians in a feather bed would envy."* (Hoyt, 1919)

Samuel Giesick, Sgt. U.S. Army Infantry Interpreter in WWI, 1917-1919   (Birdsong W. J., Photo of Samuel Giesick, Sgt. U. S. Army Interpreter WWI 1917-1919, 1920s)

As the war ground to a halt in 1918, the doughboys, including our Uncle Samuel, began preparations for their return home. In Hoyt's book, a particular passage captures the spirit of the Americans in France at the end of the war and the military stand-down and final return to our homeland. *"A year before they had seen France, lived, eaten, and some had lost their lives, in its mud. They were ready to return...*

It was better that the soldiers be returned as soon as possible. The breach between the Americans and the French had widened, and in the chasm across which they gazed there was to be found no common interests and sympathy. Lafayette had been repaid, but the thanks of the French were expressed in increased prices to the soldiers. The mass of the soldiery never understood and never forgave... The 137th Infantry and 130th Field Artillery arrived in the harbor of New York on April 23. Practically all of the organizations on the way to Camp Funston, Kansas, for demobilization, paraded two cities of Kansas and Missouri (Kansas City, Kansas and Missouri are the same metropolitan area). Short work was made of the demobilization... The men were given their discharges, their pay, and the sixty-dollar bonus due every discharged soldier of the army." (Hoyt, 1919)

A search of newspaper articles provided a few particulars of how and when the 137th Infantry was transported from France back to the United States. The *Atlanta Constitution* on Wednesday, April 16, 1919, reported the following: *"Washington. April 15. ---Additional units of the 35th (Kansas and Missouri National Guard) divisions are en route home. The war department today announced the sailing of transports carrying the complete 137th Infantry and detachments of the 130th field artillery and the 139th infantry regiment of the 35th... The transport Manchuria is due at New York April 24 with the 137th infantry complete; base hospital No. 49."* The article further detailed each unit of the 35th Division and the transport it was on. With roughly 25,000 troops and equipment sailing from Brest and Marseilles, there were nine named transport vessels carrying these men home to the seaports of Boston,

New York, and Newport News, Virginia. (Atlanta Constitution, 1919)

Through my research, I learned that the good ship Manchuria was a former Pacific mail steamer that had traveled between Hong Kong and San Francisco on many voyages. My knowledge that this was the ship that boarded the men from C Company comes from two sources. The first is the Haterius book, *Reminiscences of the 137th U.S. Infantry* (page 202). Secondly, I was shown a memento photo of the *Manchuria* by Great-uncle Samuel's grandson, Craig Crossland, which his grandfather had passed down to his family. In his description of the USS Manchuria, Haterius comments on the conditions of the transport: "*The compartments had all been taken out and bunks three high were crowded together, each section of three, two feet apart. It was somewhat crowded with 4,771 officers and enlisted men aboard. Also had some of the fairer sex on board, but–they were for "officers only."* (Haterius, 1919)

The Manchuria was on her tenth voyage across the Atlantic when the men of the 137th Infantry came aboard. The USS Manchuria (ID 1633) ultimately crossed the Atlantic on 13 round trips, of which 9 were made after the armistice, ferrying approximately 40,000 troops. She was built by the New York Shipbuilding Company of Camden, New Jersey, and was launched on November 2, 1903, remaining in service until she was scrapped in Savona, Italy, on January 12, 1952.

This momentous World War I event honored General John J. Pershing and his pledge to place a million men in France quickly. America ushered 48 divisions of roughly

28,000 men each into Europe (over 1,200,000 troops) before the end of the war. It is now known that the United States of America, in a very short time, completely re-engineered the entire rail system throughout America, appropriated hundreds of seagoing ships, and implemented a draft that sent combatants from our heartland to Europe without losing any of them to submarines or other means in the crossing.

Part III: Raising the Family

Chapter 6 ~ A Start in Hoisington

A Fresh Start

It entirely escaped me or anyone in the family to discover how my grandfather and grandmother actually met. Unfortunately, I never thought to ask her while she was alive. My father, their first son, Hiram Monroe (nicknamed "Seedy"), told us that his mother Martha was training and working to become a nurse's aide at the only hospital in the north end of Hoisington, Kansas, after she had graduated from Otis High School. Otis is about 12 to14 miles west of Hoisington. The period would have been the beginning of 1918 to 1920. My father surmised that grandfather was living with Walter and Louise White while working as a fireman out of the Hoisington Missouri Pacific Terminal (1920 Census). He probably joined friends around the railroad Young Men's Christian Association (YMCA), as did many other young people who worked out of the roundhouse (established in 1912). Grandmother Martha aspired to be a nurse's aide at the Lind Hospital, so they may have begun seeing each other at that time. It is hard to speculate what they did in their spare time, as I am not sure if the YMCA allowed women on the premises. I suppose church socials and Sunday services were a safe bet for places to meet. Hoisington is not a large town (it can be walked from one end to the other in a short time), so crossing paths would not be difficult.

The railroad YMCA was written about in *Kansas Trails,* and the following description at the time (early 1900s) was issued*: Another institution of which the people of Hoisington and Barton County are justly proud is the Railroad Young Men's Christian Association which is a branch of the International Y. M. C. A. and was established in Hoisington in 1902. The money for the work was obtained by private subscription, donations by the Missouri Pacific railroad and Miss Helen Gould. The building is in the center of five 25-foot lots on the main street of Hoisington in close proximity to the M. P. depot... The reading room is nicely furnished and on the tables are found scores of daily and weekly papers, magazines and periodicals all of which are for the free use of members. The library contains twelve large cases filled with 2,000 volumes that cover every subject for entertaining and educational reading... The lobby is large and is used by the members for playing chess, checkers, etc. The institution is not intended for railroad men alone, but contains on it membership rolls a large majority of the men of Hoisington. The membership averages around 600 but at times, the list contains as many as 800 names.*

In addition to the privileges mentioned above, at frequent intervals the members are given the benefit of lectures on practical subjects in the auditorium or assembly room. (Kansas Trails Web Site, Peggy Thompson)

It is not known when and where Martha was living when she started training and working at the Lind Hospital and Training School. This hospital was state-of-the-art, started by a very capable doctor and minister of the German

Lutheran Church. It was known as one of the better facilities in the area, according to the history of Barton County in the *Kansas Trails* narrative.

The Lind Hospital and Training School was established by Rev. W. J. Lind in the city of Hoisington and was thrown open to the public in February 1912. It is a general hospital for the treatment of medical and surgical cases and is one of the best equipped institutions of the kind in this part of the country. The building, which is three stories in height, is located in a most desirable spot in the northwest part of Hoisington with eight blocks of the business section... The building of this hospital was due to the fact that Dr. Lind, while a minister of gospel, has always been interested in the treatment and cure of diseases of the human race. He was born near the Ural Mountains in Russia, April 11, 1881. He came to America in 1902 and spent the first year after his arrival in travel during which time he visited all parts of the United States and Canada. In 1903, he entered the Concordia Seminary at Concordia, Illinois. He finished his studies at this institution in 1910. At the conclusion of his studies he was ordained a minister of the German Lutheran church... Dr. Lind spent two and a half years in the study of medicine in the old country before coming to America...

In connection with the hospital, a training school has been established under the supervision of the superintendent of nurses, assisted by a competent corps of physicians. The course comprises three years, which will render them thoroughly qualified to receive a diploma. While the didactic work is carried on in the classroom, the pupil nurse has every possible chance to study her chosen profession in its practical lines by personal contact with the different phases of her work... (Kansas Trails Web Site, Peggy Thompson)

Herbert and Martha married on September 20, 1923; I have not discovered a marriage certificate or newspaper clipping announcing their nuptials. My father remembers a couple of places they lived in Hoisington and told me he was born in the house behind the Texaco Station on Second (2nd) Street, which would have been the 200 block (West) on First (1st) Street. Herman and Hun Skolaut, my father's good friends while growing up, later became owners of this Texaco service station. Dad clearly remembers that the family lived at 665 W. 3rd Street when he was a child, until the early 1930s when they moved to 263 W. 3rd Street, across the street from the Methodist Church. He remembered the 1929 Model A Ford they drove until they moved to the 263 W. 3rd Street address, where they traded up for a 1936 Plymouth. They drove this vehicle until most of the children in the family were in high school.

In my father's 1941 senior year of high school, his father Herbert acquired a 1940 Buick Century. Though it was a brand new vehicle, it was considered a "holdover" because it had not been driven (and, of course, had not sold) when it first arrived at the dealership in 1940. I am not sure what the automobile market dynamics were at this time, but small-town America and the world was about to change forever due to wars raging around the globe and their effect on commerce. (Birdsong H. M., 2010)

The Birdsongs 1933 (1929 Model A Ford in background) (Birdsong W. J., Photo of the Birdsongs, 1933), left to right: Robert, Hiram, Dwight, Herbert Monroe, and Mary Lou Birdsong

Grandfather Herbert, after starting a family, continued to work for the Missouri Pacific Railroad out of the Hoisington terminal (Depot). My grandmother, a homemaker and mother, began raising her family in small-town America. The Missouri Pacific was one of the larger employers in the immediate area, and it was strategically located in accordance with company plans.

Hoisington (64 miles west of Salina)... A lucky town geographically because it's located in the heart of both the wheat belt and the oil territory of Kansas, Hoisington was first known as "Monon," probably from the town company of the same name which helped lay out the village. The original settlement had been established before the Missouri Pacific (then the Kansas and Colorado Pacific) was built through here. In 1886, a new town company obtained a charter for a town, purchased the land from the first company, and called it "Hoisington" after one of the partners in the company.

Hoisington is a strategic operating headquarters on the Missouri Pacific between Kansas City and Pueblo, Colorado. (Missouri Pacific Railroad, 1950)

Grandfather Hiram made regular trips from Hoisington to Horace, Kansas, and back. Horace is located on the Colorado-Kansas border near a small town, Tribune, Kansas. A book by the Missouri Pacific Company titled, *The Empire That Missouri Pacific Serves,* heralded Horace:

Go west, young man, go west." This oft-quoted advice from the famed Horace Greeley inspired the Kansas Territorial Legislature to name a county on the western border of Kansas, "Greeley," and to attach his given name to the town of Horace for that county.

Founded in 1886, Horace is located in a farming and vast prairie area. It is a shipping point for substantial volumes of cattle and grain. (Missouri Pacific Railroad, 1950)

My father tells me that his father Hiram had a small cabin (hut) that he used on every trip to Horace. He eventually inherited or purchased this place from his mentor and father-figure, Jake Crane, an older Missouri Pacific engineer who taught Grandfather Hiram the tricks of the railroad trade. Evidently, it was not much of a house in that it did not even have running water, but it was a place to get out of the weather and sleep during the many layovers that Grandfather Hiram made to this part of the Great American Desert (as Kansas was known in earlier times). To have drinking or bathing water, they had to bring water into the house in containers.

High School Days

As my father remembers, his mother and father promoted good grooming even though he did not have many clothes while growing up. Frugality ruled their closets. The clothing they owned was washed, pressed, and neatly folded. My father remembers that during his high school years he had only one older suit, which was a hand-me-down. It was near the time of Pearl Harbor and the start of the war in the Pacific that he remembered his parents deciding he needed a new suit for an upcoming school dance, and later, his high-school graduation. Therefore, they decided to go to the big city and shop for a new suit for my father.

Grandfather Hiram drove Dad to Hutchinson, Kansas, to shop for a new suit. That was the large metropolitan area of those times, and it had more choices for men's clothing. Dad wore his older suit that day, which turned out to be a good thing. They arrived in the big city of Hutchinson early in the morning. After shopping for a while they made a choice that suited grandfather's pocketbook, and he finalized the purchase. Dad was asked if he wanted to wear the new suit home and he declined, so the suit was wrapped and packaged for the ride home.

On the ride home, they traveled west into Great Bend, Kansas, on old Highway 96. As they were approaching the first intersection on the east end of town, a woman had stopped her car at the stop sign to their left. Dad remembers they were traveling 40 miles per hour because their 1936 Plymouth had a big, round speedometer in the middle of the front dashboard where both passengers in the front seat could plainly view it. The woman obviously did not see them and proceeded north into the westward flow of traffic—and into grandfather's Plymouth, smashing into the left front part of the family car.

Dad remembers only that they were traveling 40 miles per hour, but later was told that their Plymouth had rolled three times. He remembers coming to consciousness later in the backseat and noticing that the doors were locked. Seatbelts were not a safety feature, or even thought of during these years.

Dad told me that he remembers a man approaching the front window of the car and yelling something to the effect of, "I'll break the glass and get you out," which prompted my grandfather to unlock the door, push it open, and crawl out. He later revealed that he did not want glass all over the inside of the car; for fear that it would cut him and my dad.

Grandfather then crawled back in to retrieve his son from the back seat. Dad had a small cut on his forehead, which was minor, but nothing seemed to be wrong and he felt like he was OK. Upon getting out of the Plymouth, they collected themselves and determined that everyone involved in the wreck was okay. In these days, people went to a hospital only if someone was unconscious or not ambulatory. Dad marvels that he was riding in the front and ended up in the backseat, and to this day does not know how that happened. The new suit was undamaged, but the older suit that Dad was wearing had received minor abrasions.

The next day Grandfather had to drive back to the Barton County Sheriff's office in Great Bend to file an accident report. Dad tagged along. While my grandfather was filing the report, a man came in and vociferously started telling the sheriff that Grandfather had run into his girlfriend and that it was not her fault. Obviously, she had told her boyfriend that it was Grandfather who had hit the car. The Sheriff pointed to grandfather filling out paperwork and said, in effect, "You'll have to talk to that man over there..." Grandfather Hiram immediately got up and told the man what had happened—that his girlfriend was wrong and had run into them as they were traveling through the intersection, and that she had caused the accident. The sheriff verified what Grandfather had said, and my father told me, "The man left there with his tail between his legs." (Birdsong H. M., 2010)

Dad told me that after all was said and done; they went to get a five-cent hamburger on the way home, which was a special treat in those days.

Working on the Railroad

According to my father, Hiram M. Birdsong, his father worked almost all of the jobs involved with the locomotives

187

and over-rail transport of goods, services, passengers, and marketable commerce such as hauling grain, cattle, and foods. He did not work in the roundhouse or on the road or rail gangs maintaining right-of-way, but he knew many men who did, as Hoisington was a major maintenance depot halfway between St. Louis, Missouri, and Denver, Colorado—hubs of interstate commerce from east to west.

So it was that my grandfather began working during the zenith of our nation's main transportation industry, soon to be replaced with newer technology. Unbeknownst to him, the Technological Revolution had debuted into the twentieth century. Railroads were, as George H. Drury, put it in his *Historical Guide to North American Railroads*, providing prompt and safe movement of parcels, money, and goods: *One enduring symbol of railroading's past is the red-and-white diamond herald of the Railway Express Agency (REA). Today one finds reminders of REA only at museums or old depots, but it once was a major element of the American scene -- the FedEx of its day.* (Drury, George H.)

Railroads played a major role moving men and materials of the American Expeditionary Force to seaports during the First World War. *During the war, the government took control of the railroads to solve problems caused by lack of skilled labor—much of the rail peacetime work force was in the Armed Forces—and lack of capital to invest in equipment and personnel. This experiment in government control of the railroads cost taxpayers about $2 million a day. The railroads were returned to private ownership in 1920.* (Hallberg, 2009)

Based on railroad history accounts from 1929 to 1940, the Great Depression exacted a heavy toll on this industry, forcing many railways into bankruptcy. I heard many stories of hard times from both my parents and my grandparents. In fact, my parents to this day still exhibit habits that exemplify thrifty behavior learned during the Depression era. One was considered extremely fortunate to have a job, especially in such an important occupation as the railroad. It was, as I learned from my grandparents and parents, crucial to put forth an honest day's work for one's employer. Honesty was taught in all aspects of daily life, especially in work situations. It was important to a person's well-being in the community and their ability to provide for their family. And so it was with my grandfather, grandmother, and their siblings—it was just understood. Because of the hard economic times, there were specific rules and regulations set forth by the Missouri Pacific Railroad—rules that affected many lives. My grandfather, I have heard, carried a railroad regulation and rule book with him at all times and could recite most rules and regulations by heart.

In 1944, when America began to come out of the Depression, my Grandfather Hiram was involved in a train wreck in which his locomotive ran into another train. According to my father, there had been three consecutive train wrecks in a two-month period. One man was killed in the first accident (Grandfather was not involved), and the management demanded that serious attention be paid to all of these situations. They decided they would fire my grandfather.

It is important to know that the MoPac headquarters was in St. Louis, and the Division heads were not involved in the day-to-day operation in the Hoisington area. Not being close enough to the operation to understand what had actually occurred, they made a summary decision to set an example and my grandfather the target of that decision.

After being let go, he worked at odd jobs, did some carpentry around town, and filed with the Union to lobby for his reinstatement. After a three-month period, the Union steward secured a hearing with Division management and scheduled a meeting with the top man of his division.

During the hearing, the boss looked straight at my grandfather and told him, "You have been involved in a lot of accidents and destruction of company property."

My grandfather, not intimidated by any man or situation, looked the head man eyeball to eyeball and said, in effect, "Sir, please pull my file and you will see that you not only have the wrong man, you will see that I have had only one accident, and then look at my work record, and you will see that I am one of your better employees." Hiram then explained the circumstances of the accident and what had actually happened. The head man left the room to pull grandfather's file so he could read it, while he was thinking about what Grandfather had told him.

Grandfather's boss reinstated him into his regular job and told him he was sorry. He said he should have looked into the situation more fully. Grandfather went back to work but received no back pay for the time he was idle, waiting for his hearing with Missouri Pacific Division management. (Birdsong H. M., 2010)

Through the Railroad Retirement Board, I received confirmation of Hiram's pay records. It is noted that grandfather's pay was for nine months of 1944, with no pay for September, October, and November of that year. This confirms the timeline of this incident, as the records from all other years indicated that he had received his full pay.

Anyone who has worked around heavy machinery knows the dangers. You can never be too careful. Almost everyone who has worked around mechanized power equipment has experienced an accident, whether major or minor. One time Grandfather, according to my father, hooked the middle finger on his left hand on a steam lever in the locomotive engine cab. The finger appeared at first to be mashed, but later became infected and caused Grandfather to be off duty for approximately one or two months. It ended up that he had to travel by rail to the Missouri Pacific Hospital in St. Louis to receive treatment. Missouri Pacific provided health care for its employees during these times, but employees and their families had to travel to St. Louis for anything major. In Grandfather's case, the doctors amputated this finger due to complications. (Birdsong H. M., 2010)

The Hoisington-to-Horace "Trip"

I remember my grandfather taking me for short rides on a steam locomotive from the Hoisington Depot. We would head west down the tracks for a few blocks, going very slowly, until we encountered my Grandmother Martha, who was waiting for Grandpa to hand me down to her before he started his run to Horace, Kansas. This was a huge event for me at the time; I distinctly remember the experience. I must have been all of four or five years old.

I have tried to imagine what it was like to work on the locomotives—to rev up the boiler and propel that "iron horse" across the prairie into the wind. This thought has produced powerful visions within my mind—of the elation of total freedom, a surging mental thrust toward the unknown into this vast and open land. Going to Horace was, to me, like visiting one of the Seven Wonders of the World. Whenever the subject of my grandfather's trips to Horace comes up with my family, it conjures heroic visions in my mind of strong, purposeful men performing manly work. Knowing that my grandfather was part of that Hoisington-to-Horace run is a memory I hold dear to this day.

Many times, I have had my own boys in the car, driving alongside the railroad tracks as a diesel locomotive passed or kept up with our vehicle. I repeatedly encouraged my sons to put their little fists out the window and pump it up and down to see if the *ghost of my grandfather* will toot the horn on the lead engine. It has worked more times than not if we had a locomotive, chugging down the line. What a Hoot that was to observe these little guys, delighting in getting the attention of those men on those mighty Iron Horses.

Photo from Grandmother Martha's B&W Photo Collection circa 1940s (Birdsong W. J., Photograph of Grandfather Herbert's Iron Horse, 1940s)

To recreate a semblance of what my grandfather did on the Hoisington-to-Horace local trips, I researched the Missouri Pacific Historical Society and found an excellent article written for the *Eagle,* a quarterly publication for its membership, operating under a 501(c)3 charter for the preservation of MoPac educational and historical data. In the fall 2007 edition I found this article, which describes the turn-around local from Hoisington to Horace, Kansas, a trip taken in 1978 by Charlie Duckworth. This fine article provides an idea of what the trip was like for my grandfather.

The local's purpose was to keep the various industries switched between the two-crew change points. The designation for the westbound local was L603 and its eastbound counterpart was L604. The primary focus was switching the grain elevators of various size, construction, and capacity along the route. The business routine was simple: spot empty covered hoppers in the elevators on the westbound trip and pull the loads on the returning eastbound train...

Our first westbound stop was at Arnold, Kansas, where two system empty covered hoppers were placed into Huxman Dubbs Elevator. The next stop was our destination, where we tied up at Horace for the evening. The town of Horace had an interesting beginning, where in 1886 when the Denver, Memphis & Atlantic Railway was building through western Kansas. The railroad wanted to build a roundhouse and yards at Tribune, Kansas. Unfortunately, water in this part of Kansas is not a common resource, and the Tribune city leaders did not want the railroad to monopolize the supply and asked the railroad to build the facilities elsewhere. The railroad ended up building the shops and yards at Horace, two miles west of Tribune...

Horace, being close to Tribune, never really grew outside of a YMCA dormitory (built in 1912) for the crews laying over, a few small houses, the depot, a cafe that was subsidized by the MoPac, and large concrete grain elevator. While most of the crews slept in the dormitory, several trainmen lived in sod huts built in the ground around the yard during the layovers (This was the case with grandfather's and Jake Crane's little hut built of lumber). The YMCA had a separate bedroom for railroad officers...going to bed around 10:00 p.m. to get ready for the trip back to Hoisington in the morning. I believe our call time was 7:00 a.m.

As I tried to get to sleep I quickly realized my room was next to the crew's entertainment room, where a poker game was in full swing. After listening to the various "hoops and hollers" from the winners and whiners for a few minutes, I decided sleep was pretty much out of the question and got dressed to watch the festivities. The game broke up a couple of hours later and everyone headed for bed. Around 5:30 a.m. I got my wake-up call (loud rap on the door) and got dressed and headed for the cafe for breakfast. I had the owner/cook also prepare me a sack lunch with ham sandwiches to take along on the trip back...

Before departing Horace, we waited on one of the yard tracks for the KP (Kansas City to Pueblo) through freight to clear the mainline. We then left with our two GP's (Diesel Locomotives), a non-revenue JTTX flat car going to shop, and our caboose. Our first stop was Leoti, Kansas, where we pulled loads of wheat from one of the many elevators situated in the small community. The local then pulled into the siding at Ranch and the dispatcher had arranged a meet with an empty coal train. The MoPac nicknamed these "Cowboy Coal Trains" due to the Colorado mine origins. We arrived at Shields, Kansas, some 52 miles east of Leoti and pulled a load from G&W Grain Company. One hundred and thirty-four miles later the train stopped at Bison, Kansas, and picked up three loads of wheat from the large CO-OP elevator. We arrived at Hoisington and I thanked Harry and the crew for an enjoyable two days. (Duckworth, Charlie, 2007)

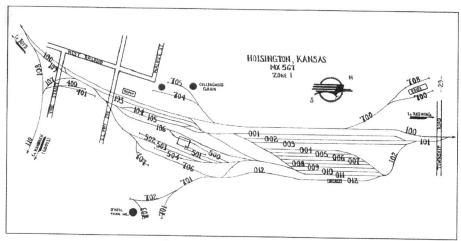

Track Map of Hoisington, Kansas.

Missouri Pacific Railroad Yard & Depot Layout ~ Hoisington, Kansas (Duckworth, Charlie, 2007)

According to Charlie Duckworth's article and what I heard from my father, the Railroad Cafe was open year-round, and the railroaders could get meals and sack lunches or dinners to go for their trips. The menu was basic bill of fare, but the food was very good.

**Missouri Pacific "Railroad Cafe" ~ Horace, Kansas
(Duckworth, Charlie, 2007)**

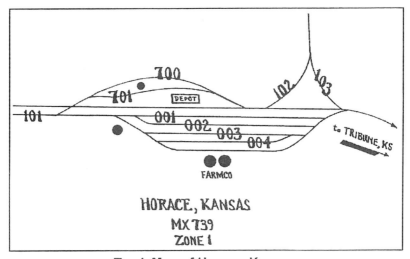

Track Map of Horace, Kansas.

**Missouri Pacific Railroad Yard & Depot Layout ~
Horace, Kansas (Duckworth, Charlie, 2007)**

Grandfather made this trip many times accompanied by
his grip, an old fashioned briefcase for carrying personal
items. In it he carried a change of clothing for the layover at

Horace, his toiletries, and the infamous fruitcakes he loved so dearly—which would as he termed it, "Tyyde [Tide] me over," until he returned. I remember pretending with the grip as a young child. I think we kept it for a number of years. It was a wonderful memory.

My father tells of the time that Grandfather sneezed his false teeth right out of the steam locomotive cab, clear into the bar ditch on a run to Horace. It happened as the trip was beginning and the engine had not gained a full head of steam. He had not yet reached the first major crossing at Otis, Kansas. He was so sensitive about not having the teeth firmly embedded in his mouth that he immediately shut down the engine to search for the missing odontoids. Surprisingly, he found them. As one might expect, his fellow workers mercilessly teased him about this incident for many years afterward. Obviously, his right-hand man, the fireman, had leaked the story.

I can remember when my *"Gram Pa"* would make a funny face at me and then somehow eject his false teeth toward me with his tongue. At first, it scared the *bejesus* out of me. He delighted in my response. After a few times of being terrified of this spirited gesture, I recognized that he was entertaining me and came to thoroughly enjoy it, begging him to do it over and over again.

At this juncture, it is important to address time—time as grandfather knew it, time as referenced with keeping time with a clock. Having and keeping a good watch was very important to railroad men, as it was the essential, most important aspect of remaining on schedule. A little-known fact is that time was not universal until railroads quilted the nation together with their vast rail network in the 1800s.

Prior to the late 1800s, every city and town across America had its own time determined by the sun. For example, when it was noon in Washington D. C., it was 12:08 in Philadelphia, 12:12 in New York, and 11:51 in Lynchburg, Virginia. When it was noon in Chicago, it was 12:31 in Pittsburgh, 12:24 in Cleveland, 12:09 in Louisville, 11:50 in St. Louis, 11:27 in Omaha, and 9:05 in Sacramento. This made it very confusing for the railroads and for people who used the railroads to coordinate with one another...

This all changed in 1883. At a meeting of an association of railroad officers (the General Time Convention) on October 11, 1883, Standard Time was adopted. The plan was for five time zones -- four in the United States, and one in the Eastern Provinces of Canada -- based on mean sun times on the 60th, 75th, 90th, 105th, and 120th meridians west of Greenwich, England. The new Standard Time was implemented on November 18, 1883. This system was established in U.S. law with the Standard Time Act enacted in 1918. (Hallberg, 2009)

My father related to me that my grandfather had to keep a watch, and that periodically he would take it to a jeweler downtown to have it calibrated and certified. He then had to turn in this certification to the Missouri Pacific Administration for verification. He also told me that Hoisington was on Mountain Standard Time (MST) for the purpose of the MoPac, even though Hoisington is located in the Central Standard Time (CST) zone. I am not sure why that time-zone format was used, but no doubt there is good logic behind it from a perspective of a keeping-on-schedule work mentality. Grandfather used both Ball and Elgin-brand pocket watches in his work. Repeatedly, my father stressed the importance of keeping a good watch and making sure it kept correct time. To this day, I set my wristwatch with the Greenwich Mean Time (GMT) atomic clock down to the nearest second.

Another tool used by the locomotive engineers of that era was to count the telephone poles as they passed them. It was common to count 40 telephone poles in every mile, which allowed Grandfather to use the secondhand on his pocket watch to gauge how fast his locomotive was going. Grandfather told my father that when he pulled the *Eagle* (a passenger train named for providing quick service between St. Louis and Pueblo), he would make his run or trip in 3 hours and 59 minutes from Hoisington to Horace and would lay over for the return trip. It was regulation that an employee had to layover for a minimum of eight hours.

There was a lot of pressure on engineers to keep on schedule, and Grandfather told dad he sometimes had the *Eagle* locomotive running up in the 100 mph range. Due to an increasing agriculture population and railroad crossings in western Kansas, the Missouri Pacific instituted a strict regulation of no more than 79 mph maximum speed on any of their trains. I am not sure of the year that rule was instituted, but guess that it was in the 1940s. My father also told me about the "dead-man" lever on the diesels. This lever was designed for the engineer to have his foot on it at all times. The rules dictated that you could not put something heavy on it and leave it. The fireman would step on it to relieve an engineer so that he could use the toilet. It was designed as an auto-shutdown lever, which would disengage the drive train of the engine.

According to Duckworth, "The Mopac had several Eagle trains: the Missouri River Eagle, Texas Eagle, and Delta Eagle. The one that ran between St. Louis and Denver (the MoPac ran it from St. Louis to Pueblo and the DRGW [Durango & Rio Grande Western Railroad] took it from Pueblo to Denver) was the Colorado Eagle."

One time a locomotive ran into and killed a man as he crossed the tracks in his vehicle at Olmitz, Kansas. It was speculated that this man wanted to commit suicide. Since Grandfather was riding in the caboose and the train was *deadheading* back to Hoisington on a return trip, he helped remove the body from the lead locomotive before they could move the train to its next destination. It was a traumatic experience for my grandfather, who came home sickened over this particular incident. My father indicated that the memory apparently stayed with my grandfather for a long time. (Birdsong H. M., 2010)

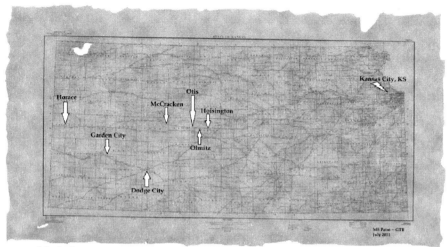

Hoisington to Horace Area of Operation on MoPac (Birdsong G. T., Hoisington to Horace Area of Operation on MoPac, 2011)

The Hoisington Ice House

It is important historically to tell of the Hoisington Ice House operation because it describes not only the cooling techniques that were so important in the preservation of food items and the keeping of essential food staples fresh for longer periods of time, but it also conveys a slice of the story of everyday life in the small towns of Kansas during these times. It was this methodology associated with the railroads that introduced carrying supplies of fresh foods throughout all of America during this period. In earlier times, livestock was either smoked or packed in barrels of salt for shipment. Shipment of live animals by rail was very costly; by the time they arrived and were butchered, about 50 to 60 percent of the meat was inedible. Cattle drives added to the cost of beef and were time consuming. Therefore, in the early 1900s dairy, poultry, fruit,

202

vegetables, meat, fish, and seafood, along with manufactured food, traveled in iced box cars on the railroads and made its way to everyday households throughout America. This next sketch of local history describes transport methods of goods, and the various technologies which were utilized during these times.

In Hoisington, Kansas, the Hoisington Ice House was necessary to the Missouri Pacific trains coming through with loads of perishable items, such as vegetables and fruit. Anything that needed to be refrigerated was serviced by the ice plant located next to the 100 track (shown on the Hoisington-to-Horace area of operations map) and feeder rails of the Hoisington Depot. Large shippers such as meat packers, breweries, and produce suppliers demanded that the railroads use this method to ship their goods to market. Robert Glynn, a WWII veteran, career army sergeant major, and native son of Hoisington, Kansas, remembers working at the ice plant as a young man and noted, "I imagine the plant was built to provide service to producers who provided perishable products on a market to market basis (west coast to east coast, vice versa and in between). While having no knowledge about the actual building of the plant, I know that the Prairie Icing Company contracted to serve American Refrigeration Transit (owners of the refrigeration box cars used to transport perishables)."

Robert (Bob) has firsthand knowledge of this operation because he worked for the plant manager in the early 1940s:

Mr. Gilstrap was the manager (principal in charge) of Prairie Icing Company...and I worked for Mr. Gilstrap as an Ice puller (manufactured and removed ice from the brine tank). A Mr. B. A. Irish was the main engineer during the beginning of the plant and had retired when I began working there in 1943-44...and the engineers at that time were Mr. Charles Ericks and Earl Lane. Mr. Prather and Poland were the American Refrigeration Transit representatives and would ensure the hopper lids were opened for icing the cars (boxcars). The trains would pull off the main line onto the siding adjacent to the extended dock. The length of this side rail extended for about the distance of one block east to about Maple Street. There were different types of trains coming through, requiring ice and each might be unique as to time for icing and leaving the dock. I would call them 'local' and 'express' (my words of description). An example of a 'local' would be melons from Rocky Ford, Colorado, which would receive its initial icing at Hoisington. An 'express' would be cars with fruit "highballing" from the west coast, was immediately iced, and then sent on its way for destinations to points in the eastern United States. (Glynn, 2010)

Bob described the facility as self-standing, meaning that it was a privately owned, profit-oriented entity dependent on market demand. He described the physical facility having a front dock, a large refrigerated storage area of two to three levels, and an office area. The main dock area was where ice was accessible to the public; it was used to load drayage trucks for deliveries to homes and businesses and to the surrounding Hoisington area. The actual plant contained the essential motors and machinery to operate the refrigeration and brine vat that froze the ice.

"There were two types of ice made while I worked there. Clear ice, which was for public use, was sold off of the front dock. And likewise it was also transported throughout the community and to the surrounding area for public consumption. The White ice was used to ice the rail cars..."

"The ice manufacturing process was both mechanical and manual. To ice a train, a 300-pound cake of ice was removed from the storage area(s) and transferred on the dock on a steel chain conveyor. The dockworkers would then start at the east end of the dock, if the train were longer than the dock. Once the icing was completed on that string of reefer cars, the engine hostler would move the train along so the remaining boxcars could be iced. When a "highball express" came in, there was an immediate crew change and without delay all of the cars were iced (or re-iced if previously iced) and the train was sent on its way as quickly as possible." (Glynn, 2010)

Bob explained that the physical process to get the ice up and on its way to the refrigerator cars was very hard work and required full concentration. As the ice was ushered up the dock via the steel conveyor chain, the workers used lance-like staffs complete with pointed spear tips and a short side hook on that spear point. A strenuous push or pull of the ice cake was all that was needed to extract the behemoth berg off the conveyor. The ice chunks coming off the conveyor were approximately six to eight feet long and were mechanically notched or indented every three to four feet. The man with the ice spear would thrust and chip at the notched areas to break the ice into more manageable sizes of approximately 50 pounds. This was done on a flat board.

Then, another man with spear in hand jockeyed the smaller chunk to the edge of the dock and onto the opening on top of the boxcars. On the top side of these reefer cars were two hopper doors (one on each end) that had been opened in preparation to receive the ice blocks. A worker would cascade blocks of ice (roughly 50 pounds) into the hoppers until they were filled. As ice fell into the opening hoppers, it would break into smaller chunks. There was some ventilation designed into the refrigeration cars, which allowed air to flow freely over the ice and cool the enclosed commodities within the reefer car for as long as the ice would remain. The coast-to-coast Highball Express refrigerator cars were inspected by both ART representatives and a Prairie Ice worker to establish a high quality standard of service.

"This process continued until ART and other companies began building new technology in refrigeration... While I worked there the company consisted of Mr. Gilstrap, the general manager, a bookkeeper/secretary, front dock workers, home delivery workers, over-the-road haulers, two engineers, three ice pullers, two dock foremen, and up to about ten train dock workers in the employ of Prairie Icing Company... I can't remember what the pay was; however, I do know it seemed sufficient at the time." (Glynn, 2010)

My father, H. M. Birdsong, remembers working at the ice house one summer in the late 1930s. He recalls that the pay was, *"75 cents if you were called in, and 35 cents an hour for icing the box cars...and you had to be there one to two hours early and have the ice on the dock waiting for when the train arrived."* He went on to say that he typically earned anywhere from six to eight dollars a week, which Mr. Gilstrap administered to him in the weekly pay. After the work was completed, there usually were raucous crap games (dice throwing), with the more experienced older men telling tales of drinking and bawdy behavior laced with colorful and explicit foul language. My father told me, "It was a fast-moving game, and some of the more experienced players would walk away with a pocketful of money." My father indicated that he was not brave enough at the time to participate (and wanted to hang onto his hard-earned cash), but he did observe this strange game. (Birdsong H. M., 2010)

Another native son of Hoisington also describes his recollections of working at the Ice House. Joseph E. Johnson, also a veteran of WWII, describes, *"Helping my dad deliver ice to homes and stores in Hoisington soon after graduating from the eighth grade. I was paid $12 dollars per week, which was a princely sum for a 13-year old—or at least I thought so. The following summers I swept the floor and kept the equipment clean in the plant... worked the front dock which is where people would get ice to take home or on a picnic. Many automobiles then had no trunk so the ice was placed on the back bumper... The Royal theatre [movie] was cooled with ice. We would haul several 300 lb. blocks of ice to the alley behind the theater, open the hatch and push blocks of ice inward... I often wonder what they did when the ice plant shut down."* (Johnson J. E., 2010)

Joe further reinforces how the average family kept food in their homes during the 1940s. *"In the forties, many homes had ice boxes (ice block type). Some had refrigerators that were broken... with no parts during the war. A block of ice in a large pan (inside the refrigerator) did the job. Restaurants and drug stores, which by the way all had soda fountains, bought ice as ice-making machines were not yet available...so the ice company sold considerable amounts of ice to the residents of Hoisington and surrounding communities, but it was a very small percentage of the total output [of Prairie Ice Company]."* (Johnson J. E., 2010)

Joe recollects that in the days before the Prairie Ice Company, much of the perishable foodstuffs from the Southwest and West were transported to the eastern parts of the United States by the railroads. He tells of the days before mechanical refrigeration, when ice was cut from lakes during the winter months and stored in warehouses to be used in insulated railroad cars. Hoisington was one of those waypoint-icing stations along the rail route, and Lake Barton was used for that purpose in the early part of the century.

He also writes that when the Prairie Icing Company finally built and outfitted the ice plant to manufacture ice, it had at the heart of its output four huge gas engines towering almost eight feet in height. Two 4-cylinder engines and one 2-cylinder engine that powered the large ammonia compressors were used to freeze the vats of water into ice and cool the warehouse ice storage area. Another 4-cylinder engine powered the electrical (alternator) power for the plant. These engines were all powered by natural gas. The ice tanks held the equivalent water which, when frozen, would produce a 300-pound chunk of brine-cooled ice. Every 15 minutes, these clusters would be pulled from the brine and sent to their destination. Joe recalled that this ice plant could produce about 100 tons of ice in a 24-hour period. (Johnson J. E., 2010)

As I researched railroad refrigeration techniques, it became apparent that many different techniques have evolved over the years. For the purpose of this book, I will show the pertinent timeline of low-temperature technology that applied during the time my grandfather worked on the Missouri Pacific Railroad, which pulled these most valuable loads of commodities. Ice apparently was the lowest-cost element used and maintained its presence in this market until approximately the 1960 to 1970s.

1913: The number of thermally insulated railcars (most of which were cooled by ice) in the U.S. topped 100,000.

1925–1930: Mechanically refrigerated trucks entered service.

1930: The number of refrigerator cars in the U.S. reached its maximum of approximately 183,000.

1936: The first all-steel refrigerator cars entered service.

1946: Two experimental aluminum-body refrigerator cars entered service on the Pacific Fruit Express; an experimental reefer with a stainless-steel body was built for the Santa Fe Railroad.

1950: The U.S. refrigerator car roster dropped to 127,200.

1957: The last ice bunker refrigerator cars were built.

(Wikipedia, 2010)

The Perfect Place to Grow Up

In the early to mid-twentieth century, most of America consisted of small towns and cities. Only in the East and on the coasts had the population centers grown in large numbers. Few mid-continent population centers had assembled large masses of people in the early 1900s. Throughout Kansas, most towns were farm-to-market centers of commerce. They were agriculture based, and in some areas oil drilling and production had made its debut. For the most part, the railroad was the link to the rest of America. Interstate commerce in large part had not fully developed, but was about to burgeon into a more fluid state of trade and transaction. Hoisington, Kansas, was one of those towns that grew up out of agriculture and needed to ship its surrounding crops to primary, secondary, and final markets.

The passage of people and goods through this small community via rail and roadway brought many different personalities and cultures to this once-vast expanse of prairie grassland. For the most part, it was a wholesome place for finding work, raising a family, and worshiping God. It was a place to pursue life, liberty, and happiness to the fullest extent. It was where my grandfather and grandmother began their lives together and started their family. I have many fond memories of this town where I spent my early childhood years, and cherish the fact that I was able to grow up where my grandparents made possible my fortunate passage into life. I am proud that I came from these roots and did not get lost in the masses of metropolitan cities. While I am sure there are some pluses to growing up in large metropolitan areas, I am happy with my birthright on the prairie.

My grandparents lived in a small home on 3rd Street in Hoisington and raised their children there. The address was 263 West 3rd Street. It was modest, but as my sister Rhea Lou (Birdsong) Heskett recalls, "*It was a huge house in my child's mind, with a big front porch and a huge back yard that had room for a tire swing behind the garage area... A clothesline seemed to go on forever, especially when the sheets hung out flapping in the breeze. There were steps down from the back porch which were perfect for picture-taking... There was a garage that seldom had a car in it but was a wonderful place to explore and hide within.*" (Heskett, 2010)

I viewed it in the same vein as my sister and spent many happy hours roaming from the front part to the backyard around this familiar place. It was the site of many cowboy and Indian skirmishes, and all the great wars were fought and won right there on that "hallowed ground." It was on a "skirmish line" in the front lawn that my best friend, John Stephan Simmons, and I decided we would become soldiers and fight for our country when we were old enough. Sadly, John was killed in Vietnam during the TET offensive of 1968. Unbeknownst to me, I was there at the same time in the northern part (I Corps area) of this strange country with the Marine Corps.

In addition, through this childhood passage, it was in this house that I discovered there was no Santa Claus. Every year my parents hired a man named Ray Smith to come to the house on Christmas Eve dressed in Santa attire, white beard included. On that glorious night when he finally came to our house, he exultantly announced his entrance at the front door by vigorously jingling the sleigh bells that were attached to a large leather strap. We would eagerly open the front door. He would then, in a jolly and raucous manner, say, "Merry Christmas!" and start bringing in the many baskets of toys and presents from the porch into the front room. We were overwhelmed with glee at this ritual. It was a joyful and happy event that my younger sister and I anxiously looked forward to each year.

One year my sister and I jointly decided that we would wait to greet Santa and help him bring in the many baskets of presents and Christmas gifts right off his wonderful sleigh while the reindeer pranced and waited for him. Although we had not yet seen his reindeer or even his sleigh, we wanted to help. We waited anxiously on the side of the house, a wait that seemed to take forever. We could visualize Santa with his magnificent reindeer and shiny red sleigh spiraling down from the sky and settling on our roof. We felt it was worth the wait.

We were, as I remember, chattering away and getting cold even though our parents and grandparents inside the house had not discovered us missing. It was exhilarating knowing that we would soon be able to see Santa and his whole operation, from the tip of Rudolph's red nose all the way to the presents in the back of his sleigh. This was real and high adventure for me and my beloved sister.

Being a bit giddy with excitement, I decided to check out the front of the house just in case I might have missed something. I was shocked that even though Santa had not arrived, his many baskets of presents to us children were already there at the front steps. Could it be that he had dropped them off, hurriedly went to another house before visiting us, and would be back to attend to my sisters and me in short order?

We decided to hide again on the side of the house and wait. Soon enough, Santa came walking and weaving down the sidewalk. My recollection was that Santa was drinking or chugging something out of a small bottle. Perhaps it was his cough medicine? Before he reached the front steps, he began to shake his sleigh bells vigorously. I looked all around and up on the roof to see if I could see his reindeer, but could not see Rudolph, any of the other reindeer, or even his sleigh anywhere.

Always a hopeful child, I decided to see what the rest of the process would be. After all, I could have been mistaken about where Santa parked his sleigh...

It was this Christmas evening in the early 1950s that I was counseled by my parents not to tell my little sister Barbara what I had seen that evening or to let her know that there really was not a Santa Claus (even though there really is—in spirit). In addition, it was this night that I received my first lesson about the Christmas Spirit. It was in this home, my grandparents' beloved house, that my sister's and my first passage of childhood innocence arrived and went *poof*!

Later, I learned this tradition was a common occurrence in many households around Hoisington, and that Mr. Smith was the premier Santa of Hoisington for years. I loved that man, as I am sure many children did. He brought hope and joy to young children all those years. May God be with him eternally as he was "the bestest of Santas" and certainly provided one of my fondest of childhood memories, which later paved the way for me to learn the real spirit of Christmas. I cannot let it pass that my sister still reminds me that I used to compliment her in those days by blurting out from time to time, "Sisser, you are a fine boy!" I am glad she was at my side that night when we discovered the spirit of Christmas.

We lived with my grandmother in her house for what seemed a long time. The reason that comes to mind is that I can remember the Christmas when I finally received what I had always dreamed of since I was old enough to know about it, which must have been as early as four or five years of age. I must have been eight or nine years old when my dream finally came true. I had been wishing and dreaming for a real BB gun.

I finally got my fine prize one special Christmas morning after getting up quite a few times during the night and sneaking into the front room to see what had appeared under the family tree. I had perfected this tactic many times throughout my young childhood. Then, on that special Christmas morning, there it was—a Daisy Red Ryder Lever Action BB Gun. I was, in my parents' eyes, finally old enough to have and handle a real BB gun. This was the dream of a lifetime for me. I was ecstatic with joy, and overeager to shoot my very own, lever-action saddle gun.

It came with a steel entrapment target, which meant that for every BB that hit that special target, the target would recapture the BB, and I could reload them back into this lever-action *BB Slinger.*

This was perfect, as I had been reading in school about the legendary William Tell, who had been exceptionally good with a crossbow. As the story goes, in the olden days he defied the royal authority and refused to bow before the royal hat on a pole in the town square. Arrested for not bowing to this authority—to this hat—Tell was forced to shoot an apple off his son's head to appease authorities. If he did not, he would be executed. If he was successful, he and his son would go free. Tell expertly sliced the apple in half and became a local hero in the eventual uprising, which he inspired.

This tale inspired me to rise above the neighborhood fold and become an expert shot with my Red Ryder lever-action BB gun. I envisioned that I would be looked upon favorably now that I had my saddle gun, but I needed to practice. With a few of our neighborhood friends looking on, I talked my sister into standing in front of the garage door with that steel target on her head and allowing me to shoot a bull's eye inside the target. If I succeeded I would be the "king shooter" on the block, the "Red Ryder BB Gun William Tell" of Roosevelt Grade School, and the all-around shooting champion of our neighborhood cowboy and Indian territory—namely, the yard and alley behind grandmothers' house.

My adoring sister readily complied with my wishes. She wanted to please me, as all faithful sisters wish to do for their brothers. From the 15-foot distance, it took only one shot from my pristine, shiny, brand-new BB gun to make a permanent indentation right between my sister's eyes before all hell broke loose. Yelling, screaming, hollering, spitting,

215

sputtering, and cry-screaming at the top of her lungs, she ran to my mother. Needless to say, my dreams were instantly shattered, and I was immediately convicted of a crime worthy of a good butt-paddling.

It was almost a year before I got my hands back on that BB gun. My dad and mom were very unhappy and distraught with my antics and took the gun away from me that Christmas day. This was the beginning of a deeper understanding of the learning process, which strengthened my *passage* toward the concept of personal responsibility.

I was the first grandson of Grandfather Hiram and Martha. Though we did not live with them in my early childhood, we eventually moved there to live with my grandmother after Grandfather passed away in 1950. I have many fond memories of my grandparents, especially my grandmother because I was her favorite, the first of many grandchildren. I cherished that pedestal she placed me on, and only later did I become aware of the tetchy feelings it caused among my many relatives and cousins. It was wonderful to be loved by my grandmother, but I eventually grew to know that I was not especially adored by the others. Such is life in both small and large towns. More importantly, my sisters have forgiven me. The casual reader will not be disturbed.

I loved those years of living in Grandmother's home. Their house was located across the street from the Methodist church we attended. The elementary school was about a block and a half west on 3rd Street. My sisters and I attended that school for most of our growing years and walked to school most every day, even in the cold and snow.

I remember coming home at lunchtime. Though my parents always told me I did not remember a lot from my really early years, I remember being on the front porch of this house with my Grandmother Martha. I was in a crib, and together we watched a thunderstorm as it passed through the neighborhood. I distinctly remember the lightning striking close to the house, which startled and scared me. It was the first time I became aware of that startling noise. Grandmother called it the "potato wagon." She often would say, "The potato wagons are rumbling," as the storm came through. I suspect this saying came from the old country and that earlier generations used it to soothe a young child's fear of that unsettling noise. The saying has stayed with me, and I have used it with my own children.

I also vividly remember going down to the pool hall (about three or four blocks away on Main Street), striding alongside my grandfather and watching him play dominoes or rummy with his friends. I would always look forward to that because he would invariably buy me a Dr. Pepper soda pop, and I would watch him engage and jest with his friends and fellow workers on his days off. He would tell everyone that I called the soft drinks "Dokor Peckers," and he delighted in having me blurt that out every chance he got. Sometimes he would buy me an ice cream cone, sherbet, or chocolate on the way home to "tyyde" me over before supper. This did not endear him to my grandmother or mother when I came home with the remnants of those cones splattered all over my face and clothing.

According to my father, Grandfather was an excellent card player. He would play for money with his friends and other patrons at the pool hall. It was said of him, "He had that deck of cards memorized and could count a deck upside down and sideways." Grandfather was an outstanding rummy player and dabbled with dominoes. I remember him lining up those chips and making them fall onto one another across the table in a serpentine array, just for my amusement. Dad told me that Grandpa kept his daughter Mary Lou supplied with pocket change that way, but Grandmother Martha considered it gambling and was vehemently against it. (Birdsong H. M., 2010)

To this day I am fond of pool halls, with the dark lighting, the smoky air, the raucous laughter, the smell of beer, and that crack of the billiard balls being pocketed in a corner pocket of a snooker or pool table.

Though he was not a drinker, the pool hall was one of my grandpa's favorite worlds away from his work. His other love was to go fishing in the creeks (or *cricks,* as spoken by the locals) in the central Kansas area where he fished for catfish. He was an accomplished *noodler.* That meant he could immerse his hand and arm into the river or creek on a deep bank or bend in the stream and slowly move his hand back and forth to simulate fish moving about or swimming. While feeling for a catfish, he would suddenly grab one with his fingers, locking it through the gill with his thumb and forefinger and then yanking it out of the water. According to my father, my grandfather did this quite frequently on his fishing trips to local rivers and streams. This method of fishing still is common in some areas of the South today.

My grandfather was a neat and tidy man who would always dress in his best clothing when he wasn't working.

My mother heard from Grandmother Martha that when my youngest sister, Barbara Jean, was born, my grandfather had just come home from a trip. He took a long bath, shaved, dusted himself with baby powder, and put on his best suit and tie in preparation to see my littlest sister and her entry into the world. Grandmother Martha had told him, "You didn't get that excited when your own kids were born!" My mother has laughed about this story for years, and she often tells of it when the subject of Grandfather Hiram comes up in conversation. That comment about my grandfather reveals a lot about his character, and I know it pleased my mother to hear about it.

My father tells of the time when the family traveled north of Ellsworth to picnic and fish on the Saline River. They all were in my grandparents' Model A Ford, riding down a shaded lane, which had trees on both sides that seemed to him almost like a tunnel. He said it seemed to stretch for a long way, perhaps a mile or more. There were some I.W.W. men (transients) resting in the shade and walking along the road. One of them jumped on the running board, exclaiming, "I'll just ride down into the town." Grandpa Hiram immediately stopped the Model A and casually displayed his personal pistol, which he always carried, and told him to get off the car. My father said the man jumped off instantly. He recalled that Grandpa told him (in effect), "If I let you ride, all of your friends will want to jump on and ride and as you can see, I have my wife and children with me and I can't let that happen." Obviously, grandfather was not afraid to act on impulse. My father said he remembered that word of this incident traveled ahead quite fast that day. As the car proceeded down the road, the men moved completely away from the vehicle. Grandfather was the quintessential family man. (Birdsong H. M., 2010)

Grandmother Martha raised a large family for the times. There were four children, beginning with my father Hiram Monroe, and then my Uncle Bob (Robert Thayne), Mary Lou (the only daughter), and Dwight Crandall (nicknamed *Red,* the youngest and only one with red hair). From hearing many stories about my father and his siblings growing up, I deduced that my grandmother was busy making sure all the children were fed, had clean clothes, and made it to school. My father confirmed that she was a serious-minded mother who would not tolerate much horseplay. I had also deduced that after listening to her life stories.

My grandmother did find time for some culture in her life. I came across an old photograph that my mother saved for me; it was of townspeople posing for the local photography studio (Peugh Photo) during the presentation of the musical and comedy play, *Plain Jane.* According to a note on the back of the photograph, Grandmother played the character Beatrice. McElbert Moore and Phil Cook wrote the original Broadway play. It debuted in New York City in May 1924 at three Broadway theatres: the New Amsterdam Theatre, the Eltinger 42nd Street Theatre, and the Sam H. Harris Theatre. It was notated on the back of the photograph that a local woman, Mrs. Kirkpatrick, directed the Hoisington presentation on February 25, 1938. The high school auditorium was the only place in town that had a stage with curtains. I suspect the performance of this play was high drama and created notoriety with the local townsfolk.

Town Play Cast of *Plain Jane*, February 25, 1938. Martha Birdsong, fourth from left, cast as "Beatrice." (Birdsong W. J., Photograph of Town Play Cast of Plain Jane, February 25, 1938, 1938)

Grandmother was a member of the Hoisington Lodge and the Rebecca Lodge, an organization that became known as "Odd Fellows." The symbol of the fraternity has three links that stand for Friendship, Love, and Truth. It was one of the first fraternities to include both men and women when it instituted the *Rebekah* degree in 1851. The name *Rebecca* (an alternate spelling) comes from the Old Testament chapter in which Rebecca draws water from the well for others, including animals. Rebekah is considered to be a protector of the water and thus, symbolically a protector of life. This organization is still in existence and focuses on the sick, charity for youth, education, remembering war heroes, and establishing homes for senior members and orphaned children. I am not sure how deeply involved Grandmother was in the Odd Fellows organization, as I did not hear much about it, but I do know that she enticed my mother to join the organization in the 1950s when we lived with her. Mother told me that she joined because of Grandmother and didn't become too involved with it.

My sister, remembers that Grandmother played in a kitchen band for a while and recalls, "I never saw or heard her band, and it was hard for me to imagine what sounds could be made from items out of a kitchen. It seems like Grandmother Birdsong's band instrument was a washboard. All I knew was that she was always excited about going off to get together with her gal friends to play in that band, and I knew that I wanted to do the same thing when I grew up since she seemed to have so much fun doing it." (Heskett, 2010)

I remember that we had an old-time washing machine and sometimes on sunny days Grandmother would have the associated washtubs outside in the backyard. The washboard was part of that set of tubs, and I remember that it looked worn. I can recall her scrubbing items of clothing on that old washboard and exclaiming, in effect, "This is the only really good way to wash clothes." Afterwards, she would hang the wet wash on a clothesline and let it flap in the breeze. In those days, everyone had a clothesline in their backyard. I remember the good feeling of putting on sun-dried clothing after it had come off the wire clothesline. Nothing felt better, including the sheets on our beds.

My sister and I often reminisce about Grandmother Martha; in our conversations, the details of our home at that time and the old memories come alive. We both agree that the grandparents' house always seemed warm and inviting. Besides our grandmother being there, our own mother was there sewing, ironing, cooking, and cleaning house, which created that security we so fondly remember. There was the dark-wood dining room set that my sister recalls was never used except for holiday dinners with family. She added that, "During the 'off season', that dining room set made a wonderful play area when we could convince an adult to let us use sheets or blankets to throw over the table to create a tent. Then we had our own little-kid world underneath that table, but we weren't supposed to scratch the furniture." (Heskett, 2010)

We often have laughed about the radio, which my sister says was "fashioned into a piece of furniture" in the living room. As I remember, it was the centerpiece for family get-togethers. As my sis recalls, "We sat around the radio in the evening as an incomplete family, since our daddy was always working or sleeping, and we listened to radio programs. To this day, I only remember the Amos and Andy Show... However, I do have a recollection of that radio generating news of the Korean War because my Uncle Red was in that war, and my grandmother was distraught and feared her son may have been in the event announced on the news. Luckily, my uncle returned home from Korea, and my sister and I were his favorite little children." (Heskett, 2010)

These memories stimulated my thought process, leading me to remember the many evenings that we sat around listening to that radio. I recall that I always tuned to the *Lone Ranger and Tonto.* "Hi yo Silver and away!" was my call to action in my play stage outside, and I reveled to hear the Lone Ranger blurt out that phrase on the radio before galloping away on Silver, his trusty horse. I always wanted a friend like his sidekick Tonto at my side.

The many days we spent in that beloved house on 3rd Street seemed endless at the time. We especially looked forward to the one day each week when Grandmother did baking and we could watch her perform her magic. I fondly remember the many pies, cakes and tasty breads she baked. Bread was my favorite, and I would enthusiastically eat the leftover dough bits. I loved it when she allowed me to lick the spatula and clean out the cookie-dough batter in the bowl as she put the cookies on the baking sheet and placed them in the oven. My sister and I would fight over who would get the first licks. My sis remembered, "As a little girl, I do not remember being hugged or cuddled by Grandmother Martha, but when she fried up scrap noodle batter and pie dough scraps and sprinkled sugar and cinnamon on it, that was just as good as a hug from Grandmother. It seems like our mother never wanted her to feed us that treat. Maybe our mother did not want our appetite spoiled before supper, as she knew what happened to us kids when we had too much sugar. But I loved it when Grandmother Martha forged ahead and let us eat her fried goods anyway." (Heskett, 2010)

My sister also recalls that two of Grandmother's brothers, who lived nearby in Otis, Kansas, always came to visit on special occasions. Both were successful wheat farmers and were proud Volga-Germans. Every Labor Day there was a celebration with a parade and a carnival, which was set up in the lower downtown area of Hoisington. Each year on Labor Day, my sister and I would sit eagerly on the front steps until other relatives (Uncle Sam, Aunt Ella, and Great-uncle Charley and his wife, Aunt Elsie) arrived. They were our favorite great-aunts and great-uncles. While waiting on their arrival, we observed the neighbors, their children, and other townspeople walking by our house on their way downtown. My sister Rhea would get envious and worry that "they were going to get ahead of us and take in more of the events or get to see more than we would."

When everyone finally arrived, we would walk downtown to watch the parade and then go to the carnival. When Uncle Sam finally arrived, he would take us aside, pull a dime out of our ears, and give it to us. This seemed extraordinary to me, as I could not understand how he performed that wonderful gesture by simply looking into my ear. He claimed that he saw something in there and touched my ear with his rather large fingers, and miraculously finding a ten-cent piece in there. We loved his generosity and would put that sacred ten-cent piece in our pockets for the carnival, or sometimes just save it in our piggybank. We always thought Uncle Sam was rich. As we later learned, he *was* a rich man in his religion, spirit, and character and he had a rich *passage* through life.

There always seemed to be a crowd in Grandmother's backyard, usually we had a game going or were staging a make-believe event. I'll never forget the alluring hammock ride that we children rigged in the back of Grandmother's yard, dangling the hammock between the clothes pole and a large tree. Picture, if you will, a canvas shroud stuffed with old wool blankets to enlarge it. It was adorned with an old Mexican high-back saddle that had been stripped of its leather. This creaky wooden frame of a saddle with a metal saddle-horn was secured loosely onto the middle part of that drooping hammock. We would happily mount it and urge both our friends and enemies to try to dislodge us from this make-believe bronco riding perch. They would do so by savagely see-sawing and zig-zagging the end ropes of the hammock from both ends.

It was a tremendous challenge to ride a make-believe rodeo ride for as long as one could, without the politically correct bike helmet that so many young kids wear today. I would get knocked silly and almost unconscious by that imaginary bronco, but would get right back on it as I was not about to let anyone know that I was hurting. In those years, having the time of my life was more important than letting anyone know I had gotten the crap knocked out of me.

When we finally got the event really going and everyone was having an exhilarating time, Mother or Grandmother would shut it down when someone would run home screaming and yelling at the top of their lungs shortly after getting bucked off and landing on their head. I am still amazed that no one broke their neck or was impaled by that metal saddle-horn.

Then there were the light shows in the late evenings on the front porch of Grandmother's house. She taught my sisters and me the art of watching a thunderstorm in all of its many stages. We witnessed them at her Brother Samuel's farmhouse northwest of Otis. On the prairie, we could clearly see glorious and majestic thunderheads for miles. Light shows were the evening's buildup of thunderstorm clouds, flashing brilliantly in the distance, illuminating with bright momentary flashes and reporting seconds later with shocking booms (which I imagined were from cannons). They were ethereal visions of ever-changing mountains, white and gray in color, billowing and cascading, performing their nightly act in the play on the prairie theatre. They were, as generations before ours termed, "the artillery of heaven." We learned to sit quietly on the porch and view these satisfying and awesome displays of God's work, letting our minds wonder what our Lord in his heavens had in store for us in days to come. Those evening buildups were, I suppose, presentations of hope for many a wheat and grain farmer on that vast prairie of western Kansas during those times. The final act of those presentations sometimes brought a gentle and soothing rain. I am still, to this day, an avid theatre patron of light shows.

The Last Trip to Horace

I remember my formative years in that small town of Hoisington in the heart of Kansas with profound fondness, recalling the warmth, comfort, and security that surrounded me and my family. One could say it was an idyllic childhood, being raised by caring parents and coddled by doting grandparents. Nothing in life is forever, and the one thing that is certain during our *fortunate passage* through life is change. Change came to me in my fifth year of life when I learned that Grandpa was in serious condition in the hospital in Garden City, Kansas. I vaguely remember thinking that he was going to be all right, not fully comprehending or understanding what was wrong with him. A child's mind has not yet accumulated the experiences of life's traumas, and a young mind is almost totally filled with hopeful, wholesome, and good thoughts. The idea of a loved one leaving has not yet entered one's world at this stage of life.

Grandfather boarded the train in January 1950 and made his last trip on that mighty iron horse to Horace, Kansas. My father told me that Grandfather was not feeling well that day. Evidently, he made the trip to Horace and had a layover. On the return trip, he turned the engine over to his fireman at Leoti, Kansas, leaving the train so he could search for a doctor. The depot dispatcher loaned him his car, and Grandfather drove to Scott City, where he unexpectedly ran into his older brother, Jim. Dad said that Grandfather was in so much pain that he did not recognize his brother. Jim then took him to a doctor in Leoti. The physician determined that Grandfather needed to go to Garden City Hospital, which was better equipped to care for him.

I heard that the doctor himself drove Grandfather to the hospital in Garden City. Grandfather walked up three flights of stairs to get into a hospital bed. According to my father,

Grandpa lived 13 days from the time he got off the train in Leoti, Kansas on January 13th, a Friday, and departed into eternity from his passage in the world on January 25, 1950. He had suffered a ruptured appendix. I am not sure of the details of the surgery, but our family doctor, Doc Brown from Hoisington, went to Garden City to see what was going on. He was upset over the procedure, saying to my dad that if he had known about it, he could have saved our beloved grandfather. He said the problem had something to do with the proper cleaning of the internal area, organs, and drainage. (Birdsong H. M., 2010)

I distinctly remember going to see my grandfather in the hospital. He had tubes inserted in his nose. I thought to myself that it looked like green beans were coming out of his body through those hoses. I assume now that it was the poison being extracted from his stomach-colon area. I remember thinking that he was going to be all right and would return to us after he got well. This was the last time I saw my beloved grandfather, and I remember him telling me something like, "Be a good boy." My sister was with me, and he comforted her. I often think of him being in the ethereal (heaven) and looking down upon me as I have gone into the different passages or phases of my life. The thought of him looking over me from above is comforting and has helped me in my decision processes. I visualize him looking down when I take that right fork in the road and always thank him, knowing that he is pleased. On the other hand, I hope that he was not watching when I took some of those wrong forks in the road during my passage.

Following are entries from the Family Group Chart of the Herbert M. and Martha Birdsong Family.

Husband	Herbert Monroe Birdsong	
Birth	Nov. 11, 1895	Pleasant Hill, Talbot Cty, GA
Marriage	Sep. 20, 1922	Ellsworth, KS
Death	Jan. 25, 1950	Garden City, KS
Burial		Hoisington, Barton Cty, KS
Other Wives		
Parents	**Dr. James Christian Birdsong** and **Mary Lou Weaver**	

Wife	Martha Giesick	
Birth	Aug. 10, 1901	Otis, Rush Cty, KS
Death	Nov. 29, 1993	Aurora, Colorado
Burial		Hoisington, Barton Cty, KS
Other Husbands		
Parents	**Adam Giesick** and **Maria Kathrina Hergert**	

Children		

1	Hiram Monroe Birdsong	
Gender	Male	
Birth	Jan. 3, 1923	Hoisington, Barton Cty, KS
Wife	**Winnie Jean Webb**	
Marriage	Dec. 28, 1944	Blackwell, OK
Death		
Burial		

2	Robert Thayne Birdsong	
Gender	Male	
Birth	Sep. 20, 1924	Hoisington, Barton Cty, KS
Wife	**Shirley Hanson**	
Marriage	Jun. 20, 1948	
Death	Apr. 15, 2002	Denver, CO
Burial		

3	Mary Lou Birdsong	
Gender	Female	
Birth	Oct. 12, 1927	Hoisington, Barton Cty, KS
Husband	**Wendell S. Kenyon**	
Marriage	Oct. 19, 1946	
Death		
Burial		

4	Dwight Crandall Birdsong	
Gender	Male	
Birth	Aug. 15, 1930	Hoisington, Barton Cty, KS
Wife	**Ramona Bisbee**	
Marriage	Jul. 11, 1954	Bucklin, KS
Death		
Burial		

Family Group Chart, Herbert M. and Martha Birdsong Family, Hoisington, Barton County, Kansas, 1900s

230

PART IV: THE GOLDEN YEARS

Chapter 7 ~ Golden, Colorado—Last Stop

My Grandmother Martha ended up in the Denver area and finally in Golden, Colorado, in her final years after leaving Hoisington to follow family to Colorado. She first went to Sterling, Colorado, in 1954, to be close to Robert, her second son and his family. She worked in a nursing home at that time, and not much is known about those times. Later she followed Robert's family to the Denver area and became a dorm mother at Colorado Women's College in northeast Denver. After that, she rented a basement apartment at 4600 31st Avenue in the Sloan's Lake area from Mrs. Violet Fuller, who became a very good friend. During those years in the 1960s and 1970s, Grandmother worked for an Olan Mills photography studio. She seemed to enjoy it very much, especially when a family would schedule a photo session. She thoroughly enjoyed interacting with children. Her landlord, Violet, often gave tablecloths to my sisters when they came to visit. According to my mother, Violet had worked for the Denver Dry Goods Store and always seemed to have an abundance of those types of things. She was well known by many people in Denver from her career at Denver Dry Goods. During the 1970s, Grandmother moved into a townhome on Yank Court in Golden, Colorado, which was in a secluded area and turned out to be the right accommodation for her lifestyle.

It was in those years that she blossomed into an even greater grandmother, paying a lot of attention to her many grandchildren. I must say that she was always there for me. Even though I did not always do things that pleased her, she was a constant and solid rock of support and stood behind me no matter what. She, like my mother, lavished me with unconditional love. She saw me off to Vietnam, as she had with her sons in the earlier wars. She was a proud Blue Star Mother who had given two of her sons, a grandson, and a great-grandson to our nation's military in time of war. That to me is an honorable, humbling, and fearsome bequeathal, as I know personally what it is like to sacrifice and send a son to serve our nation during time of war. It is the highest of all honors, in my estimation.

John Stuart Mill, in his 1859 publication, *Essays on Liberty,* wrote, "War is an ugly thing, but not the ugliest of things. The decayed and degraded state of moral and patriotic feeling which thinks that nothing is worth war is much worse. The person who has nothing for which is more important than his own personal safety, is a miserable creature and has no chance of being free unless made and kept so by the exertions of better men than himself."

As they say, "Freedom is not free." I believe this nation and its liberty and freedoms will be tested again in the future. This nation and its freedoms have to be maintained or it will cease to exist. I, the grandson who joined the U.S. Marines and went to Vietnam, am extremely proud to have served my nation while others of my generation evaded or shirked their national duty. Our political leaders chose the war in Vietnam; we did not. We loyal men carried the fight to our enemy there. I never told my grandmother or others in the family about my real combat experiences in Vietnam.

I know she prayed constantly for my safe return, as did my parents. I am and will be forever grateful to all of them for their prayers.

Memories

As I recall, my grandfather carried himself like a mature and responsible man anyone would be proud to claim as a father or grandfather. Allowing my memory to meld with what I have learned of mature and responsible men over the years, without having the benefit of knowing him past my fifth year of life, it is apparent that my grandfather fit that mold. What I have learned of him and his life has given me license to surmise what I think could be said of him, coupling that with what is known about him to build his legacy so I can pass his persona on to future generations.

My fondest and clearest memories of my grandfather have been documented in this writing. He undoubtedly wanted me to know his world and the pride he had of being in daily command of that huge iron behemoth. *Strong* and *sure* are words that come to mind when I think of my grandfather. Yet, I remember there was softness in him so that I knew he cared for his whole family, including me. As I vaguely remember, he had a certain distance of manner that set him apart from other men. His best friend and mentor, Jake Crane, told my father that he (my grandfather) was one of the best on the engines, but you had to work for him, right beside him, and that there was no slacking, no rest, and no quarter given until the job was done. I truly understand what a hardworking man he was.

Another lifelong friend of Grandfather's was Fred Cuddy, a MoPac engineer who lived about a block from my grandparents. Mr. Cuddy was an avid angler and loved to comb the banks and "holes" of the winding Arkansas River south of Great Bend, Kansas. After Grandfather passed, Fred would ask my mother if he could take me fishing with him on the weekends. He had been my grandfather's fishing companion in earlier years, scouring the many haunts of the Smoky Hill, Saline, and Walnut Creek waterways. Even though my father took me on many excursions to the outdoors to hunt and fish, I also loved to tag along with Mr. Cuddy because he liked me and told me stories about my grandfather. I also sensed that he was in command of superior fishing (catfish) knowledge, having spent previous years perfecting the art alongside of my grandfather (who was rumored to be quite adapt at taking a catfish or two).

Fred always would ask my mother in advance if I could accompany him on weekends. I loved riding in his old Studebaker that he had adapted for accommodating all the fishing tackle and equipment needed for a fishing expedition on the many conduits of the muddy, sandy, and mostly slow-moving currents of those western Kansas waterways and tributaries. Some years during the spring, the Arkansas would be at the high-water mark with what was termed *runoff*, meaning that snow from the high country west toward the Continental Divide in Colorado was melting rapidly, and much of its rapid watershed would pass through this confluence. As I remember, we would drive to the banks of the entire favorite, hard to access places along the Arkansas and do the diligence of a sight survey while judging if the river was right for casting a line. It was Mr. Cuddy's judgment of the water conditions and the right amount of feeding matter in the water that captivated my interest and kept us in long question and answer conversations during those awesome outings. I was in awe of his judgment, and I remember thinking about and studying his thought process in my spare time. I now know his was a methodology of trying all things that made common sense and remembering the ones that worked. Experience is the master of which I write. I am inclined to believe that my grandfather was cut from the same cloth as his friend Mr. Cuddy, and would have cultivated my apprenticeship in those same fishing habits and customs had he been a continued part of my early life. May God bless Mr. Cuddy and Grandpa on whatever stream they are fishing now, or whichever steam engine they command up there in the ethereal?

Conversely, I was privileged to live around my grandmother most of my life. She was by the strongest of standards a steadfast woman. When I asked my family to tell me about her in a word, my mother told me that she was "strong," and my sisters recall that she was "independent," "energetic," and "outgoing." My younger sister, Rhea, once told me that, "I called her my teenage grandmother." My favorite memories of her were when we had Christmas at her house on 3rd Street. It was a time of family and joyous celebration of the Christmas season and worshipping God and his son, Jesus. Grandmother was not a zealot about her religion, but made sure that we children knew she believed in a being higher than herself, and she would remind us from time to time the meaning of reverence toward our maker. My father recalls that she took them to church frequently when they were children, and that he hated going because they always had to sit in the front-row pew.

Grandmother Martha in her later years (Birdsong W. J., Photo of Grandmother Martha Birdsong - Portrait, 1960s)

I remember, as a youngster, always feeling secure and happy when grandmother was preparing meals with my mother, as they completed the laborious task of cooking and choreographing a large family dinner where everyone would thoroughly enjoy not only the meal, but also the small talk and visits. These are some of my fondest memories.

My sisters and mother remembered that Grandmother loved the latest fashions and would order clothing from catalogs. She had sort of a fetish for mail ordering, as I recall. Of course, I knew that she was frugal, so I am positive that most of the merchandise she ordered was within her economic means. My sisters tell me they thought that Grandmother was quite fashionable, in keeping within her age group.

Grandma was a conservative woman, one of a few that I have known. She would save almost everything and neatly file it away, and could find most anything when the need for it arose. She was, in my estimation, a very good cook, but was even better at revitalizing leftovers. When we kids were growing up, hamburger was a luxury item on the menu. Grandmother could make the best meatloaf and just about anything out of a pound of hamburger. She could save most food items for what seemed like a long time, and then make them come alive and taste good when the occasion arose to resurrect a meal from the fridge or freezer. I know she was on a limited budget and would make do with the small amount of money she had coming in monthly to meet her obligations. However, she always had good wholesome meals for us when we visited, and was happy to cook for the whole family. I never once heard her complain about providing meals for anyone in the family. It was a happy time for her to be cooking for her kids and grandkids.

Grandmother was never a drinker; however, she would have a few sips occasionally with guests and at family functions when we children were grown. I remember that she had collected a collage of liquor, wine, and decorative bottles that she kept accessible for special occasions. I am told by my mother and sisters that she would save the last drops of any leftover alcohol and place that brand in the big, decorated bottle, which (like a book-of-the-month club), would be offered to unsuspecting guests or relatives who stopped by for a visit in her Golden, Colorado, townhome. I often wish I could go back as a fly on the wall and observe the serving and imbibing of those Cannon Ball cocktails.

I clearly remember when Grandmother moved into an assisted living facility. She was not the kind that would readily accept close personal assistance. She was one who had accepted the firm and total personal responsibility of her daily needs, such as fixing her own meals, caring for herself, washing her own clothing, grocery shopping, and so forth. She was without a doubt an independent woman who would not ask for help or want it in her daily existence. It was a severe setback for her to lose that independence and her ability to go and come as she pleased.

The assisted-living place was a restrictive environment. I would go get her and bring her into our home as often as I could, as she loved my children and was very interested in them and their activities. I remember bringing her home for the weekend many times.

Grandmother always enjoyed the springtime, especially when the lilacs bloomed. That was the first thing she noticed when I brought her to our home the last time. I think they were her favorite flowers. She had a passion for lilacs and always referenced them when the subject of flora came up. In almost every place that she lived, there were lilac bushes on the property or somewhere nearby; Grandmother would find them and would snip off a few stems to place around the house while they were blossoming. She loved to sit in our backyard during the lilac-blossoming period of the springtime and watch, smell and admire these transitory works of art. It was comforting for me to see her in that state of mind, sitting in a lawn chair and enjoying such a simple pleasure—reveling in the ephemeral beauty of those fleeting and fragile bushes. Every time that I see or think of those temporal, impermanent budding shrubs, I realize, as my grandmother did, that everything in life is impermanent, time-bound and passing through this world only to reappear again, reborn.

This was the beginning of the end of her life's journey, and she would amaze me by finding the simplest of pleasures to enjoy. I slowly began to realize that she was passing these passions, interests, and enjoyments to me through her observation of nature and its many wonders. They were an endowment for me and my children to enjoy when we were ready to discover what she already knew. I now understand what she intended.

In her final days, it was hard for our family to watch my grandmother slip into Alzheimer's. Her condition at first seemed to be a gentle condition of moving back and forth from forgetfulness to certified dementia. It eventually progressed into a full state of Alzheimer's disease.

During this time it was very hard to visit her, as she did not know who was there most of the time. Toward the end, she recognized no one. I remember going to see her with my father just before she passed. My parents had come to visit for a special occasion. When we entered her room, I was overwhelmed by the distinct smell of death lingering on her breath, a scent that was more than familiar to me after my two tours in Vietnam. I knew at that moment that she would not be with us for much longer in this world she had so passionately enjoyed and loved; her organs were shutting down. At that moment, I prepared myself to say my final goodbye to her as she was leaving on her next journey. I believe that both my grandparents had a good and beautiful *passage* through life.

When your grandparents and parents finally pass, you lose them in a sense, but you really do not lose them. They are forever gone from the face of this earth, but in another sense, they are still with you. They are within you, giving you guidance and providing comfort and direction every day. Their essence has not left you, but remains in your person even though they have completed their long and arduous passage. Honor them well as you undertake your own passage.

BIBLIOGRAPHY

Ambrose, S. E. (2000). *Comrades:Brothers, Fathers, Heroes, Sons, Pals.* Simon & Schuster, Inc.

Atlanta Constitution. (1919, April 16). Transports Sailing With U. S. Soldiers.

Bellware, D. A. (2003, April). The Last Battle. *Civil War Times.*

Birdsong, D. J. (1915-1917). Brothers James & Herbert Birdsong.

Birdsong, D. J. (2010). *Ancestry & Descendants of My Grandparents Dr. James C. Birdsong MD & Mary L. Weaver* (1st ed.). San Diego, California, United States: Dean J. Birdsong.

Birdsong, D. J. (2010, February). Disscussion of Family. (G. T. Birdsong, Interviewer)

Birdsong, G. (2010, Dec). USA Volga German Settlements.

Birdsong, G. T. (1887-1888). Family Group Chart.

Birdsong, G. T. (1901-1993). Martha Birdsong Homemaker. Kansas, United States.

Birdsong, G. T. (2011, July). Hoisington to Horace Area of Operation on MoPac.

Birdsong, H. M. (2010, February). Family History Interview. (G. T. Birdsong, Interviewer)

Birdsong, W. J. (1912). "Souvenir" - Students/Teachers of School District No. 48. Pioneer TWP (Township).

Birdsong, W. J. (1914, March 31). Martha Giesick Catechism certificate from Methodist Church, Otis, Kansas. *Katechismus - Prufung*. (German, Trans.) Otis, Kansas, United States.

Birdsong, W. J. (1917). Post Card of Camp Funston, Kansas Induction Process. Camp Funston, KS.

Birdsong, W. J. (1917-1920). Martha Giesick with unknown woman. Otis, KS.

Birdsong, W. J. (1918). Post Card of Semaphore Signaling Exercises - Camp Doniphan, Oklahoma. Ft. Sill, OK.

Birdsong, W. J. (1920). Certificate of 32 Degree Masonry - Herbert M. Birdsong. Hoisington.

Birdsong, W. J. (1920s). Photo of Herbert M. Birdsong. Hoisington.

Birdsong, W. J. (1920s). Photo of Samuel Giesick, Sgt. U. S. Army Interpreter WWI 1917-1919.

Birdsong, W. J. (1924-25). Photo Uncle Sam Giesick Farmhouse. Otis, KS.

Birdsong, W. J. (1933). Photo of the Birdsongs. Hoisington, KS.

Birdsong, W. J. (1938). Photograph of Town Play Cast of Plain Jane, February 25, 1938. Hoisington, KS.

Birdsong, W. J. (1940s). Photograph of Grandfather Herbert's Iron Horse. Hoisington, Kansas.

Birdsong, W. J. (1960s). Photo of Grandmother Martha Birdsong - Portrait. Denver.

Birdsong, W. J. (1987). Photo of Uncle Sam Giesick Barn and Windmill. Otis, KS.

Birdsong, W. J. (1987). Photo of Uncle Sam Giesick Farmhouse. Otis, KS.

Birdsong, W. J. (2010). Photograph of Fireman Shovel MPRR {Missouri Pacific Rail Road}. Sidney, Nebraska.

Birdsong, W. J. (Early 1900s). Photo of Adam Giesick. Otis.

Birdsong, W. J. (Early 1900s). Photograph of Ella Giesick. Otis.

Birdsong, W. J. (Early 1900s). Wheat Harvest Thrashing Machine Giesick Farm Early 1900's. Otis, KS, United States.

Board, R. R. (2011). Personnel Records of Employee's Prior Service; Railroad Retirement Board. Chicago, Illinois.

Davidson, W. H. (1983). *A Rockaway in Talbot: Travels in an Old Georgia County* (Vol. Vol. 2). Hester Printing.

Department of the Army. (1953). History of the 137th Infantry Regiment. Carlisle, PA, USA: U. S. Army Military History Institute, Carlisle, PA 17013.

DeVorsey, L. (2003). *New Georgia Encylopedia.* Retrieved October 2010, from www.georgiaencyclopedia.org.

Dr. Bernard A. Weisberger. (1967, June). Here Come the Wobblies! *American Heritage Magazine, Volume 18*(4).

Drury, George H. . (n.d.). *Historical Guide to North American Railroads.*

Duckworth, Charlie. (2007, Fall). Riding the Hoisington - Horace Local. *The Eagle.*

Evans, L. B. (1913). *First Lessons in Georgia History.* New York: American Book Co.

Figes, O. (1989). *Peasant Russia, Civil War: The Volga Countryside in Revolution, 1917-1921.* New York: Oxford University Press.

Georgia, A. (1867). Talbot County Map 1867.

Georgia, A. (1869). Upson County Map 1869.

Georgia, A. (1897). Marriage Licenses. *Marriage Register*, 193. Georgia.

Giesick, S. (1974). Letter "The Story of the Giesick Family".

Glynn, R. (2010, August). Hoisington Ice House history. (G. T. Birdsong, Interviewer) Hoisington, Kansas, USA.

Government, U. S. (1910). *Thirteenth Census.*

Government, U. S. (1915). *Kansas Decennial Census.*

Government, U. S. (1917). *Selective Service Regulations WWI.* Washington D. C.: Government Printing Office 1917.

Government, U. S. (1920). *Fourteenth Census.*

Hallberg, M. C. (2009). *Railroads In North America.*

Haning, S. (1976). *Rush County Kansas: A Century in Story and Pictures.* Kansas: Print Press, Inc & The Rush County News.

Hannah, C. W. (1930). *History of Upson County, Georgia.* J. W. Burke.

Haterius, C. E. (1919). *Reminiscences of the 137th U. S. Infantry.* Crane & Company, Topeka.

Hergert, D. (1887-1888). Family Group Chart (AHSGR Form #G-3). American Historical Society of Germans from Russia.

Hergert, D. (1987). American Historical Society of Germans from Russia. St. Paul, Minnesota, United States.

Hergert, D. (1987, August 7). Letter to Martha (Giesick) Birdsong. *Letter.*

Hergert, D. (1988, April 5). Letter to Aunt Martha. St. Paul, Minnesota, United States.

Hergert, D. (1988, September 25). Letter to Grady Birdsong. *Letter.*

Hergert, D. (n.d.). Confirmation Class Picture Otis, Kansas.

Heskett, R. B. (2010). Family History Interview. (G. T. Birdsong, Interviewer)

Hoyt, C. B. (1919). *Heroes of the Argonne: An Authentic History of the Thirty-fifth Division.* Franklin Hudson Publishing Company.

http://Oklahoma4h.okstate.edu. (2010). *Oklahoma Ag in the Classroom.* Retrieved from http://Oklahoma4h.okstate.edu.

http://www.ephesians5-11.org/hiram.htm. (2010). *Ephesians 5:11 - Who is Hiram Abiff?* Retrieved from http://www.ephesians5-11.org/hiram.htm.

Johnson, C. (2012, April). Troup County Historian. (G. Birdsong, Interviewer) La Grange, Georgia.

Johnson, J. E. (2010). Hoisington History, Roundhouse and Ice House. (G. T. Birdsong, Interviewer) Cawker City, Kansas.

Jordon, R. H. (1971). *There Was A Land: A Story of Talbot County, Georgia, and its people.* Columbus, GA.

Joseph Fort Newton, L. (Copyright 1925). *The Holy Bible - Authorized King James Version.* Oxford University Press - American Branch.

Joseph Fort Newton, L. (n.d.). *The Bible and Masonry (Preface in THE HOLY BIBLE).* New York, London, Toronto: Oxford University Press.

Kansas Trails Web Site, Peggy Thompson. (n.d.). *http://genealogytrails.com/kan/barton/bartonhistory2 0.html*. Retrieved 2010, from Kansas Trails.

Karlin, A. (2010, January 17). *Volga German Immigrants in Kansas - Kansas Historical Society.* Retrieved 2010, from http://www.kshs.org/teachers/trunks/volga.htm.

Kornbluh, J. L. (1968). *Rebel Voices: An IWW Anthology.* Ann Arbor: University of Michigan Press.

Lucian Lamar Knight, L. F. (1920). *Georgia's Roster of the Revolution.* Index Printing Co.

Malin, J. C. (1944). *Winter Wheat in the Golden Belt of Kansas.* Lawrence, Kansas: University of Kansas Press.

Martin, J. H. (1875). *Columbus, Georgia from its Selection as a "Trading Town".* Columbus, GA: Thomas Gilbert, Printer and Book-Binder.

Miller, P. (2010). *Center for Volga German Studies at Concordia University.* (Patrice@Webbitt.com, Editor) Retrieved January 17, 2010, from http://www.webbitt.com/volga/gathering.html.

Missouri Pacific Railroad. (1950). *The Empire That Missouri Pacific Serves.*

Mohrland, J. (1986, January 16). *http://www.brunnental.us/brunnental/index.html.* (S. Stahl, Ed.) Retrieved January 18, 2010, from Stahl Homepage.

Nudd, J. (n.d.). *U. S. World War I Draft Registrations.* Retrieved from http://eogen.com.

Smith, C. L. (1933). *History of Troup County (Georgia).* Atlanta, GA: Foote & Davies Co.

US Army, W. D. (1919). Military Personnel Records - National Personnel Records Center. *Pay Record - War Department - Form No. 371.*

Webmaster. (2010, January 17). *http://cvgs.cu-portland.edu/origins.cfm.* Retrieved 2010, from Center for Volga German Studies at Concordia University.

Webmaster, C. (2010, January 17). *http://cvgs.cu-portland.edu/immigration/united_states/kansas/otis.cf m.* Retrieved 2010, from Center for Volga German Studies of Concordia University.

Wikipedia. (2010, September). *en.wikipedia.org/wiki/Refrigerator_car.* Retrieved September 2010, from Wikipedia, the free encyclopedia.

INDEX

251

252

CPSIA information can be obtained at www.ICGtesting.com
Printed in the USA
BVOW060653170812

298030BV00005B/3/P